HARDWARE PC

HardWare PC - Pentium III, AMD K6-3 and peripherals

Copyright © 1999 Book Express Publisher

All rights reserved. No parts of this book shall be reproduced, stored in a retrieval system, or transmitted by any means, electronic, mechanical, photocopying, recording, or otherwise, without written permission from the publisher. No patent liability is assumed with respect to the use of the information contained herein. Although every precaution has been taken in the preparation of this book, the publisher and the authors assume no responsibility for errors or omissions. Neither is any liability assumed for damages resulting from the use of the information contained herein.

Trademarks

All terms mentioned in this book that are known to be trademarks or service marks have been appropriately capitalized. Book Expess Publishing cannot attest to the accuracy of this information. Use of a term in this book should not be regarded as affecting the validity of any trademark or service mark.

Editor:
Gorki Starlin

Translator:
Patrick Dulphi

WorldWide Books

Av Americas 5001 - 207/208
Rio de Janeiro - RJ
Brazil - Zip Cod: 22631-004
Phone 055 21 325-6131 / 325-0493

Printed in Brazil

FOREWORD

Some months ago my second book on hardware called "Complete Hardware Manual
2nd edition" was launched. This book contained a large quantity of information and technical details about how peripherals function, and advanced configurations of personal computers.

Although the book received a lot of praise from professionals in this field, it's size and cost made it prohibitive for beginners and ordinary users, as well as the fact that not everybody has time to read a book with almost a million characters or have interest in the most technical details of how to configure the SETUP BIOS for example.

To fill in this gap we decided to write one more book, this time aimed at beginners and with more focus on information that is likely to be used in real life. The final result is a book with a little more that 180 pages, divided into 12 chapters, that in spite of it's reduced size concentrates sufficient information to turn any beginner in the hardware area into an intermediate level computer technician, capable not only of assembling and configuring a micro but also of understanding it's functions and resolving the most common problems.

Finally I hope that this boot meets your expectations and that you enjoy reading it as much as I enjoyed writing it.

C. E. Morimoto

Acknowledgements

Firstly I wish to thank God for all He has bestowed upon me during my life.

To Gorki Starin, director of Book Express Publisher for his support and incentive.

Dedication

I dedicate this book to my family who, though faraway, are always on my mind and in my heart. Also to all the students and friends who respect and offer incentive to my work.

Contents

#1 How the PC Works — 1
- Binary System 1
- Basic Functions 2
- Components 6

#2 Processors — 11
- *Math coprocessor* *12*
- *Cache Memory* *12*
- architectural differences 14
- Processors 14
  - *8088* *14*
  - *286* *15*
  - *386* *16*
  - *486* *16*
  - *Pentium* *17*
  - *AMD 5x86* *19*
  - *Cyrix Cx5x86* *19*
  - *AMD K5* *19*
  - *Pentium MMX* *19*
  - *AMD K6* *21*
  - *AMD K6-2* *21*
  - *Cyrix 6x86MX* *22*
  - *Pentium Pro* *22*
  - *Pentium II* *23*
- Integrated L2 Cache 24
  - *Celeron* *25*
  - *Socket 370 vs Slot One* *26*
  - *Pentium II Xeon* *28*
  - *Pentium III* *28*
  - *AMD K6-3* *29*
  - *AMD Athlon (K7)* *29*
- performance comparisons 30
  - *Integer performance* *30*
  - *FPU Performance* *31*

HARDWARE PC

#3 RAM Memory   33

   Format 34
      30 pin simm memory modules 34
      72 pin memory modules 35
      168 pin DIMM memory 36
   168 pin DIMM memory module 36
   Types of Technology Used 36
      FPM (Fast Page Mode) Memory 37
      Edo (Extended Data Output) Memory 37
      SDRAM (Synchronous Dynamic RAM) Memory 38
      PC-100 (100Mhz memory) Memory 38
   ECC and Parity 39
   How the hard disk functions 41
   How data is written and read 42

#4 Hard Disks   43

   Formatting 43
      FAT 16 44
      FAT 32 45
   Logical structures 45
      Boot sector 46
      FAT (File Allocation Table) 46
      Root directory 46
   Recovering data 47
   The Gigabyte of 1 Billion Bytes 48

#5 The Motherboard   49

   Formats 49
   Motherboard Components 50
   Diagram that shows a typical layout of the components on a motherboard. 50
   BIOS 51
   L2 Cache 52
   Processor socket 53
   54
   Jumpers 55
   Buses 55
   ISA (Industry Standard Architecture) of 8 bits 55
      ISA 16 bits 56

EISA (Extended ISA) 57
VLB (Vesa Local Bus) 58
IRQ (Interrupt Requests) 63
DMA (Direct Memory Access) 64
Plug-and-Play 65
   Problems with Plug-and-Play *66*

#6 Video cards and Monitors   69

Video Memory 69
3D Video cards 70
How it Functions 71
Monitors 72
LCD Monitors 75
How an LCD functions 77

#7 CD-ROMs, Sound Cards, Modems, Printers and Scanners   79

CD-ROM 79
DVD 80
Sound Cards 81
Generating digital sound 82
External Connectors 83
Modems 83
   Hardmodems vs Softmodems *84*
Printers 85
   Dot Matrix Printers *85*
   Ink Jet printers *85*
   Reconditioned cartridges *86*
   Laser Printers *87*
Scanners 87
Interpolation 88
OCR 88

#8 Choose the Best Configuration   91

Choose the Best Configuration 91
Choosing the motherboard 91
Choosing the other peripherals 92
   RAM Memory *92*
   Processor *93*
   Hard Disk *93*

Video Card 94
Sound card 94
Upgrades 95

#9 Assembling and Configuring   97

Beginning the assembly 98
Installing the processor 101
    Cooler clamped above a processor using a metal spring clip fixed to the ZIF socket. *102*
Fitting the memory modules 104
Fitting COAST modules 105
COAST module in place 106
Processor speed 108
What is Overclocking? 110
Processor voltage 112
    Pentium classic (P54C) voltages *112*
    Pentium MMX (P55C) voltages *113*
    AMD K6 Voltages *113*
    Cyrix Voltages *114*
    I Voltage *114*
Other configurations 114
    CPU Type Jumper *114*
    CMOS Discharge Jumper (clean CMOS) *114*
    Onboard Sound and Video *115*
    Front Panel connectors *115*
    Speaker *116*
    Reset *117*
    Keylock *117*
    Hard Disk and Power LEDs *117*
    Turbo Switch and Turbo LED *117*
    Configuring the frequency Display *118*
    HD and CD-ROM jumpers *119*
Fixing the disk drives 121
Connecting the ribbon and power cables. 122
Finalizing the Assembly 123
Plugging the Power cable 124
Connecting the serial and parallel cables 124
Fitting ISA, PCI and AGP cards 126
Finishing the assembly 127
Problem Solving 127

Other configurations 132

#10 Configuring CMOS Setup and Formating the HD   131

Advanced CMOS Setup *132*
Power Management *133*
Integrated Peripherals *133*
Security *135*
Partitioning and formatting the hard disk *135*
Formatting the HD with only one partition 138
Dividing the HD into several partitions 138
Defining an active partition 139
Excluding Partitions 139
Installing a second hard disk 140

#11 Installing Windows and Configuring the Hardware   143

Finding files 146
Installing video cards 149
Installing the Monitor 151
Installing sound cards 152
Installing Modems 153
Installing Printers 155
Installation of SCSI controllers 156
Using the Device manager. 158
Making a small network 158
Installing a network card 160
Configuring the network 160
Reinstalling Windows 161

#12 F.A.Q   163

Hard disk and Memory 165
Other Peripherals 172
Upgrade 179
Windows 182

How the PC Works

To the layman a computer may appear to be a mysterious machine, a "black box" where information is saved and processed in some mystical way.

However there is no mystery to computers. Everything functions in an ordered, and up to a certain point, simple manner. The objective of this initial chapter is to give an overview of the components of a computer and how it all functions. Later you will get to know each component in more details, learn to assemble and configure micros of the PC standard and how to go about solving problems, then you will be ready to solve your own problems, as well as those of your friends, and maybe, who knows, even work in this area.

BINARY SYSTEM

There are two ways to represent information, analogically, or digitally. Any song recorded on a standard cassette tape is analog, coded in the form of waves, that may be of an unlimited number of frequencies. Bass sounds are represented by a lower point in the wave whereas the higher points represent the treble frequencies. The problem of this method is that any interference causes distortion in the sound. If computers worked with analog data there certainly would be many possibilities of error, because any interference, however small would cause alterations in the processed data, and consequently in the results.

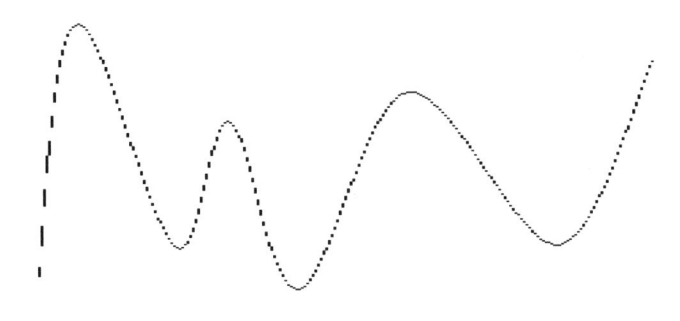

Analog signal

HARDWARE PC

The digital system however, permits storing of any information in the form of a sequence of positive and negative values or in other words, in the forms of 1s and 0s. For example the number 181 may be represented digitally as 10110101. Any data, whether it be text, an image, a program or anything else to be processed is stored in the format of a large sequence of ones and zeros.

It is exactly the use of the binary system that turns computers trustworthy because the possibility of a value of 1 being altered to a value of 0 (the opposite) is very small. The speed of processing also is much more because the computer only has to deal with two different values, making the calculations much simpler.

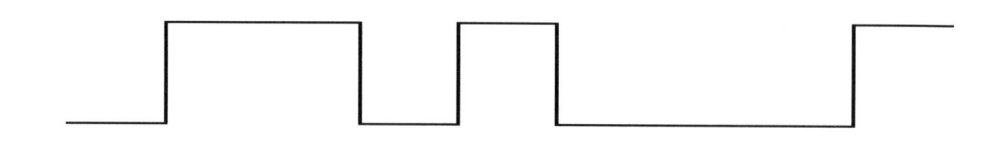

Digital signal

Each binary value is called a "**bit**", a contraction of "binary digit". A group of 8 bits form what is called a **byte**, and a group of 1024 bytes form a **Kilobyte** (or **Kbyte**). The number 1024 was chosen because it is the power of 2 closest to 1000. A group of 1024 Kbytes form a **Megabyte** (1048576 bytes) and a group of Megabytes is called a **Gigabyte** (1073741824 bytes). The next multiples are the Terabyte (1024 Megabytes) and the Petabyte (1024 Terabytes).

We also use the terms **Kbit**, **Megabit** and **Gigabit**, to represent groups of 1024 bits. Just as a byte corresponds to 8 bits, a Megabyte corresponds to 8 Megabits and so on.

1 Bit =	1 or 0
1 Byte =	A group of 8 bits
1 Kbyte =	1024 bytes or 8192 bits
1 Megabyte =	1024 Kbytes, 1.048.576 bytes or 8.388.608 bits

BASIC FUNCTIONS

The basic architecture of any computer, whether it is a PC, Macintosh or a mainframe, is formed by only 5 basic components: Processor, RAM memory, hard disk, input-output devices and software.

How the PC Works

The **processor** is the brain of the system in charge of processing all the information. However, in spite of its sophistication, the processor cannot do anything by itself. To have a functional computer, we need some more support units, such as memory, disk drives, input-output devices and finally the programs to be executed.

The main memory, or **RAM memory**, is used by the processor to store the data that is being processed, being used like a kind of work bench. The quantity of RAM memory available determines which activities the processor may execute. An engineer would not be able to produce the plans of a building using a school desk. In case the amount of RAM memory is insufficient the computer will not be capable of running more complex programs. The original IBM PC, launched in 1981 for example, had only 64 Kbytes of memory, and for this reason was only capable of executing simple text based programs. A more modern micro with at least 32Megabytes of memory is capable of executing much more complex programs.

RAM memory is capable of responding to requests from the processor at a very high speed. This would be perfect if it were not for two problems, the high cost and the fact that it is volatile, or in other words it loses all it's information when the computer is switched off.

Seeing RAM memory serves only as a kind of working area, there is another type of memory which is used to store programs and files: called **mass memory**. The principal mass memory storage device is the **hard disk**, where all the programs and data is kept while they are not being used or when the micro is switched off. Diskettes and CD-ROMs are also representative of this type of memory.

In order to understand the difference between RAM memory and mass memory you may imagine a slateboard and a bookshelf full of books with various problems to be solved. After reading the problems to be solved in the books (mass memory) the processor will use the slateboard (RAM memory) to resolve them. A soon as a problem is solved, the result is noted in a book and the slateboard is cleaned ready for a new problem to be solved. Both devices are equally necessary.

In order to permit communication between the processor and the other components of the micro, as well as between the user and the micro there are **I/O devices** (Input/Output). These are the eyes, ears and mouth of the computer, because it is through these that the micro transmits and receives information.

There are two categories of input and output devices:

The first is composed of devices that make the communication between the user and the micro. The keyboard, mouse, microphone, etc. (for the input of data), the monitor, printers, speakers, etc. (for the output of data).

The second category is aimed at the communication between the processor and the other internal components of the micro, such as RAM memory and the hard disk. The devices which form part of this category are generally to be found in the motherboard and include disk controllers, memory controllers etc.

Like all machines, a computer no matter how advanced it is, is "stupid", because it is not capable of reasoning or doing anything by itself. It needs to be told each step. It is here that the **programs**, or **software,** enter into action, they co-ordinate the functioning of the physical components, making them execute the most varied jobs, from games to scientific calculations.

The programs installed determine what the micro will "know" it is able to do. If you want to be an engineer the first thing to do is go to a university and learn the profession. A micro is not so different, however the "learning" is not achieved at a university but through the installation of an engineering program such as AutoCAD. If you want your micro to be able to draw then all you have to do is install a drawing program such as CorelDraw and so on.

All physical parts of the micro, such as processors, memory, hard disks, monitors, i.e. everything that you can touch is called **hardware**, whereas all the programs and files stored are called **software**.

There are two types of programs, so called **high level software**, and **low level software**. These designations do not indicate the level of sophistication of the programs but rather their involvement with the hardware.

The processor is not capable of understanding anything except machine language, instructions relatively simple that order the processor to execute mathematical operations like addition and multiplication as well as other tasks like reading and writing data, comparison etc. As it is extremely difficult and laborious to make the computer execute anything writing programs directly in machine language, there are small programs like BIOS and device drivers of Windows to automate the most basic tasks, functioning as intermediaries or interpreters between the other programs and the hardware. These programs are called low level software. All the other applications programs, like word processors, spreadsheets etc., are run above these resident programs, indirectly using them to access the hardware and for this reason they are called high level programs.

The **operating system** itself, of course, must not be forgotten. Tthis functions as a kind of bridge between the user and the Hardware, automating the use of the computer, and offering a sold base from which the programs can be executed.

Continuing with the previous examples, the operating system may be defined as the "personality" of the micro. A micro running Linux for example, would never be as user-friendly and easy to operate as another micro running Windows 98 as an example. On the other hand, Windows 98 is unlikely to be as stable as a third micro running Windows NT. The differences don't stop there: Programs developed to run under one operating system are almost always incompatible with other operating systems. A version of Corel Draw designed to be run under Windows 98, would never run under Linux.

The interface of the various operating systems is different also. In MS-DOS for example, we only have a command prompt, based on text, whereas in Windows there is graphics interface based on the concept of windows.

This division facilitates the life of the programmers who may concentrate on developing ever more complex applications in a shorter time interval.

To write a simple control Box program in a low level language, such as C for example would take ate least a days work for a programmer. A program with the same functions written in a visual (or high level) language would take only minutes, and would count on a much more beautiful and user friendly graphics interface. In the primordial days of computing, in the 50s, 60s and 70s, there were several manufacturers competing for market share. Each one developed its own computers which were incompatible amongst themselves, both in respect of the hardware level and software level.

In spite of executing the same basic operations, practically everything was different: The components of one could not be used in another, the programs were incompatible, and even the programming languages were different

However standardization was inevitable with the popularization of microcomputers. In the beginning of the 80s, there were basically only two different types of architecture or "families" of personal computers. The PC developed by IBM and the Macintosh, developed by Apple.

As it was cheaper, the PC became more popular, the use of Macintoshes being restricted to niches where its own characteristics made it more attractive, such as for the editing of images , sounds and desktop publishing.

As the PCs possessed an open architecture, that is to say other manufacturers could develop their own components and standards, there is a wide range of compatible components available. The user can choose the components he wants from a wide range of makes and models, choosing those that best fit his needs, and tailor make his own configuration. Also it is possible the improve the micro later on by means of upgrades, changinng some components in order to improve its performance. Even branded micros like IBM, Compaq, Dell are assembled using components bought almost entirely from other manufacturers. For example, there could be an Intel processor, Quantum hard disk, ASUS motherboard, Kingston memory, Mitsumi CD-ROM, NEC diskette drive, LG monitor and so on.

This book deals only with micros of the PC standard. But as both architectures have the same basic concepts, you, the reader, should not have any difficulties later in adapting to working with the maintenance of Macintoshes or any other architecture.

COMPONENTS

Now that you understand what is inside the cabinet of a PC, it's time to take a closer look at the function of some of its main components.

You should already be familiar with the function of the processor. There are various different processors to be found on the market. In order of evolution we may quote the 486, the Pentium, the Pentium MMX, the K6, the K6-2, the Pentium II and the Celeron, the K6-3, the Pentium III and the Athlon. In the chapter about processors you will get to know each one better.

Pentium processor

We defined the processor as the brain of the computer. Every brain has to have a body, and the mother board is exactly that.

It reunites all the components that the processor needs to communicate with other peripherals, such as hard disks, video boards etc. Another function of the mother board is to accommodate and control the voltages to the processor etc.

Each processor needs a specially developed mother board because due to the differences in architecture they have different "necessities". Each processor has a different number of contacts or pins, operates using a different voltage and needs supporting circuitry especially designed for that processor. The method of installation changes from family to family. The Pentium II for example uses the so-called "Slot 1" that appears similar to a video game socket whilst the K6 and Pentium use another type of socket called "Socket 7".

How the PC Works

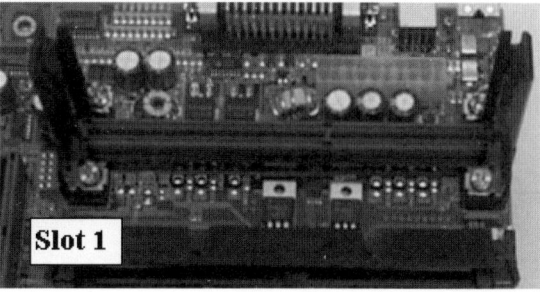

Socket 7

Slot 1

In spite of their differences, motherboards are normally developed to be compatible with more than one processor. A modern motherboard with a socket 7 for example, can normally accept processors going from a 75Mhz Pentium up to a K6-3 of 500Mhz, including in the middle, Pentium MMX, K6 and Cyrix 686. A modern Slot 1 motherboard in turn supports Pentium II, Celeron and Pentium III processors. Within this book you will learn to discover which processors may be used in each model of motherboard and how to configure the motherboard appropriately.

The importance of the motherboard doesn't stop here. This also determines which components may be used in the micro (and consequent upgrades) and has a direct influence on the overall performance of the computer. Certainly you would not like to spend $200 or $300 on a latest generation video card only to discover that you can't use it because your motherboard doesn't support it.

Slot 1 motherboard.

In order to work, the processor also needs RAM memory, which is sold in the form of

HARDWARE PC

little cards called **memory modules**, that fit into slots on the motherboard.

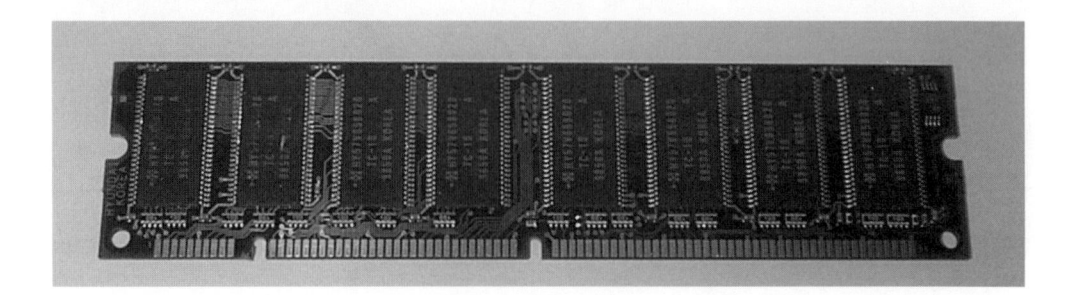

168 pin memory module

In order for the micro to save programs and other files etc, we need a hard disk drive (HD) that is installed inside the cabinet and connected to the motherboard by means of a cable.

An essential component is the cabinet, a metal Box that houses and protects the fragile internal components of the micro. This also houses the " power supply" which is responsible for converting the alternating mains current (AC) to direct current (DC) used by the majority of electric components. It also serves to attenuate small variations in voltages, thus helping to protect the equipment.

The motherboard, processor and memory are the three basic components of the micro. otherwise we would have a deaf and dumb computer, incapable of transmitting or receiving information. Now it is necessary to add sensory devices in the form of more components. The most essential are a video card, that permits the micro to generate images that may be seen on the monitor screen, and a keyboard and mouse that permit the user to operate the micro.

Other components amplify the resources of the micro, but may be defined as optional, given that the PC may function without them:

The CD-ROM permits the micro to read CDs with programs or games. In case the micro also has a sound card you may even play normal music CDs. There are also DVD drives that can play films as well as playing normal CDs.

A sound card permits the micro to generate sounds, played by a pair of loudspeakers. The sound card also has inputs for a microphone and connector for a joystick Together with a CD-ROM drive this forms the so-called Multimedia kit.

The Fax-Modem permits two computers to communicate using a normal telephone line. This means the reception and transmission of faxes, and of course, access to Internet.

There is also a diskette drive, that in spite of being a low technology device, is still used to copy data from one PC to another.

As well as these there is an enormous range of accessories: Printers, scanners (that digitise images digital),cameras (that generate digital images instead of using films), video conference cameras, video capture cards and many more.

2 PROCESSORS

We saw in the previous chapter that the processor is the principal component of a computer, but in order to have a fully functioning computer we also need to have RAM memory (to store that data wich is being processed), a hard disk (to store programs and other files) a video card and a monitor with which to communicate with the user, and finally a motherboard which contains the components, permitting communication with all the peripherals.

In case just one of these components has a low performance it will affect the performance of the whole micro, no matter how rapid the processor.

It's a waste of time trying to put a Ferrari motor in a VW Beetle. A mere K6 or Pentium MMX with lots of RAM memory, a fast hard disk and a good video card can actually be faster than a Pentium III with a weak component.

BASIC CHARACTERISTICS

There are several processors available on the market, each one with different resources and prices. To decide which processor is the best purchase option in each case is difficult, because while one processor is suitable for a specific application, it may be quite unsuitable for another.

When we buy a processor, the first thing to ask is it's operating frequency, or speed, measuring in Megahertz (Mhz), millions of cycles per second. However a processor with a higher operating frequency is not always faster than another which may have a slightly lower frequency: the operating frequency indicates only how many operations are executed each second, however what the processor is capable of doing in each operation is another story.

Imagine a processor 486/100 MHz, beside a Pentium with also 100 MHz. In spite of the operating frequency being the same, the 486 loses badly. In practice the Pentium would be at least twice as fast.

This happens due to the different architectures within the processors, and also because of the math coprocessor and the built-in cache.

Math coprocessor

All the x86 family processors as used in PCs are basically whole number (Integer) processors. However many applications need to use number fractions as well as complex mathematical functions such as SIN, COSINE, TANGENT etc, for their processing. This is the case of programs such as CAD, spreadsheets, games with 3D graphics and image processing in general. These complex mathematical functions may be emulated via software using combinations of simple instructions, however with a very low performance.

The function of the math coprocessor is exactly this, to help the main processor calculate these complex functions. As the coprocessor possesses specific instructions to execute these types of calculations, it is 30 to 50 times faster than the main processor executing the same calculation via emulation, it is an essential component.

Up to and including the 386, the coprocessor was only an accessory that could be bought separately, and installed in a socket on the motherboard, each processor model had it's own equivalent coprocessor:

Processor	Coprocessor
8088	8087
286	287
386SX	387SX
386DX	387DX
486SX	487SX
As from the 486DX	Integrated with the processor

The problem with this strategy was that as few users equipped their micros with arithmetic coprocessors the production of these chips was very low, and therefore the prices were extremely high, so that in some cases the coprocessor cost more than the main processor.

With the increasing number of applications that needed coprocessors its incorporation into the main processor as from the 486 was a natural step. With this the problem of the high cost was also resolved, as the set was cheaper to produce.

Cache Memory

Whilst processors have become almost 5.000 times faster than the 8088 (the processor used in the XT) RAM memory, its principal work unit has evolved little in performance.

When the 386 processors were launched, it was soon perceived then that memory was no longer capable of keeping up with the speed of the processors, many times the processor had to keep "waiting" for data to be freed up by memory so that it could finish its tasks, thus losing a lot of performance.

If the speed of memory was a limiting factor in the age of the 386, you can well imagine it would seriously affect the performance of the processor that we have today. Memory cache began to be used to help solve this problem, a type of super fast memory, that is used to store the data most frequently used by the processor, thus avoiding, in many cases, having to resort to the relatively slow RAM memory. Without this the performance of the system would be limited and the speed might be up to 90% less. There are two type of cache, called **primary cache**, or **L1** (level 1) cache, and **secondary cache** or **L2** (level 2) cache.

The primary cache is built-in to the processor itself and is fast enough to be able to keep up with it. A new type of cache memory must always be developed every time a new processor is designed. As this type of memory is extremely expensive (sometimes thousands of times more expensive than conventional RAM memory) only a small quantity is used. The 486 had only 8 KB, the Pentium 16 KB, whilst the Pentium II has 32 KB.

To complete the picture a secondary cache memory which is slightly slower is used. Being considerably cheaper a much larger quantity can be used. The most common was 128KB or 256Kb in the 486s whilst in todays the micros, 512Kb is common. Depending on the processor used, the L2 cache may be within the processor (like the L1 cache) or be on the motherboard.

Every time the processor needs to read some data it looks first in the L1 cache. In case it doesn't find the data the processor hasn't lost any time, given that the primary cache functions at the same frequency. In case the data is not in the L1 cache it will then look in the L2 cache. If it finds the data in the secondary cache it will lose a little time, but as not much as if it had to access RAM memory. However if the data is not any either of the two caches, there is no choice but to lose several processing cycles waiting for the data to be supplied by the slower RAM memory. For example, if you were reading a book and suddenly need some information that you had noted down on a piece of paper. If the paper was on your table, you could read it without losing much time. If it was inside a drawer of your desk, you would need some more time to find it, while if it was somewhere in the middle of a big filing cabinet on the other side of the room, it would take a lot longer to find.

Round about 95% of the time the data requested is already present in the cache in a micro with 512 KB of L2 cache L2 and 32 KB of L1 cache This is considered the optimum cost/benefit ratio by the majority of manufacturers. By adding more cache a little more performance is gained by reducing access to memory, but making the system more expensive. Adding another 512 KB of L2 cache, giving a total of 1 MB, improves the performance of the micro approximately 7%, whilst adding another 32 KB L1 cache totaling 64 KB results in an increase of about 8%. Adding cache gives a significant gain only when the system does not have any cache or has only a small quantity.

ARCHITECTURAL DIFFERENCES

Differences in the internal architecture, such as in the design of the processor and the transistors that make it up, also determine in which operations the processor will be faster.

A processor basically performs two types of operations, one involving whole numbers (integers) and one involving floating point numbers (fractions and more complex arithmetical functions).

Whole number operations are handled by the main nucleus of the processor, whilst those involving number fractions etc. are left to the math coprocessor.

Office programs, such as Word, Excel, Power Point, Internet Explorer, Netscape as well as Windows itself, use whole number processing almost exclusively. However programs that manipulate graphics such as AutoCAD, CorelDraw!, Photoshop, 3D Studio, and games that use 3 dimensional graphics (such as Quake) use principally the floating point unit.

Some types of processors are better at whole number processing (such as the K6, K6-2 and K6-3 of AMD and the 6x86 of Cyrix) , whilst others are better at floating point calculations (like the Pentium II and the Celeron). To decide in which processor you should invest your money, the applications to which the micro is destined should be taken into consideration. There is a chart showing the performance of some of these processors in various aspects at the end of this chapter.

PROCESSORS

How about getting to know some of the processors used in PCs one by one ?

8088

The 8088 was in fact an economy version of the 8086, that had been launched by Intel in 1978. IBM thought of using the 8086 when they were developing their personal computer, but the 8088 was finally chosen due to its low cost.

Both the 8086 and the 8088 were 16 bit processors, and were considered advanced for their time in spite of being extremely simple by today's standards. The difference between them is that while working with 16 bits internally, the 8088 had an external bus of 8 bits, that is to say, that in spite of processing 16 bits at a time, it communicated with the other peripherals (like disks, video cards etc.) using words of only 8 bits, permitting the use of simpler and cheaper peripherals. The 8088 was capable of accessing up to 1 Megabyte of RAM memory and functioned at a velocity of 4.77 MHz, incredible for that time.

As apoint of interest, the original IBM PC, launched in August 1981 possessed only 64 Kbytes of RAM memory, a 12" monochrome monitor, had a 5 ¼ inch disk drive with a 160Kb capacity and didn't have a hard disk. The operating system was MS-DOS 1.0. Two years later, the PC XT, was launched wich, in spite of continuing to use the 4.77Mhz 8088, had 256KB of RAM, a hard disk drive of 10MB, a CGA (Color) monitor and MS-DOS 2.0.

Even with the arrival of the 286s, the XT continued selling well because it was quite a lot cheaper. Clone makers (IBM compatibles) created XT type designs more advanced, with 8MHz 8088 processors, bigger hard disks and up to 640KB of RAM memory.

286

The 286 brought several advances over the 8088. It used binary words of 16 bits both internally and externally (to communicate with other peripherals) that permitted the use of 16 bit peripherals, much more advanced than those used in the original PC and the XT.

The main progress brought by the 286 were its two modes of operation, so called **"Real Mode"** and **"Protected Mode"**. In real mode the 286 behaved exactly like an 8088 (except faster), offering total compatibility with existing programs. In protected mode it showed its true potential, incorporating more advanced functions like the ability to access up to 16 Megabytes of RAM memory multitasking, virtual memory virtual on disk and memory protection.

Even the most modern processors still incorporate the two modes of operation. In spite of seeming a backward step, it is necessary to maintain backwards compatibility with older programs that can only be executed with the processor in real mode. All versions of MS-DOS, including DOS 7.x used in Windows 95 and 98, work with the processor in real mode.

When the micro is switched on the processor automatically operates in real mode, only operating in protected mode if requested to by some program. It is for this that even Windows 98, wich operates with the processor in protected mode, still uses MS-DOS. Actually DOS serves only to initialize the micro and leaves the scene as soon as the processor enters protected mode.

In spite of already having protected mode, the 286 brought several limitations which impeded its effective utilization. Because of this, micros based on the 286 ended up being used only to run applications in real mode that could also be run on an XT, taking advantage only of the higher speed of the 286. Speaking of velocity, the first version of the 286 functioned only at 6MHz, an 8MHz version was launched soon after that was used in the PC AT. Subsequently versions up to 20MHZ were developed.

386

The 386 brought several new resources. To begin with, the 386 worked both internally and externally with 32 bit words, and was capable of accessing memory using a bus of 32 bits, permitting a data transfer rate up to twice as fast. As the 386 could work with binary words of 32 bits, it could access up to 4 Gigabytes of memory (2 to the power of 32).

Like the 286, the 386 continued having two modes of operation. The difference is that in the 386 it is possible to alternate between real mode and protected mode freely. A 386 is the minimum requirement to run any modern operating system or application in protected mode. With a 386 with sufficient RAM memory and hard disk space you can run Windows 95 and most of its applications even though slowly due to the low processing power of the processor.

As the 386 was a 32 bit processor it was necessary to develop new motherboards to work with it which made systems based on it much more expensive and kept many potential buyers away.

To get around this problem, Intel launched a low cost version of the 386 called the 386SX wich -+in spite of continuing to function internally with 32 bit words, communicated with launched a low cost version of the 386 called the 386SX that in spite of continuing to function internally with 32 bit words, communicated with RAM memory and other peripherals using 16 bit words (like the 286). In order to differentiate the two processors Intel began to call the original 386 the 386DX. This architecture permitted the use of the same peripherals as used in 286 motherboards, making machines based on the 386SX much more accessible in price. Just to have an idea, a basic PC, equipped with a 386SX, cost less than 1.000 dollars, almost half the price of a 386DX based computer

486

Like the 386DX, the 486 worked with 32 bit words both internally and externally and was capable of accessing up to 4 Gigabytes of RAM memory. There was a large evolutionary leap in performance.

First an L1 cache of 8MB was added to the processor (the 386 had no internal cache,

Processors

only a small quantity on the motherboard) and as if this were not enough, the 486 was the first processor to bring a built in math co-processor. Summed to the changes in the internal architecture of the processor these improvements turned the 486 almost twice as fast as a 386 of the same clock speed.

As it had previously done with the 386, Intel created a low cost 486 called the 486SX, wich was identical to the original, but without the internal math co-processor. In order to avoid confusion, the original 486 was called the 486DX.

25Mhz, 33Mhz and 40Mhz versions of the 486 were launched, but a barrier was created because at that time there were no motherboards capable of operating at more than 40Mhz. To get around this problem, the concept of a clock multiplier was created, in which the processor worked internally at a velocity greater than the motherboard. Processors 486DX2 were then launched (which operated at twice the motherboard frequency) and soon afterward the 486DX4 (which operated at triple the motherboard frequency). The operating frequency of the motherboard is called the **BUS FREQUENCY**.

Processor Velocity	Motherboard velocity (bus frequency)	Multiplier
486DX-2 50 MHz	25 MHz	2x
486DX-2 66 MHz	33 MHz	2x
486DX-2 80 MHz	40 MHz	2x
486DX-4 75 MHz	25 MHz	3x
486DX-4 100 MHz	33 MHz	3x

As only the speed of the processor changed, it was possible to develop "Upgradable" motherboards that permitted a DX33 to be replaced by a DX2-66 or a DX4-100 for example, simply by changing some jumpers on the motherboard.

Another novelty brought by the 486 processors was the necessity of a cooler (ventilator) on the processor to avoid excessive overheating. A cooler must be used on all processors from the 486 DX-2 and above.

Pentium

Like the 486, the Pentium is a 32 bit processor, capable of accessing up to 4 Gigabytes de RAM memory RAM. The Pentium however, brought several improvements over the 486, that made it almost twice as fast as a 486 of the same clock speed. We can emphasize the increase in the L1 cache, that became 16KB (double that of a 486) and a completely redesigned math co-processor, almost 5 times faster than that found in the 486, making the Pentium faster still in applications that require a great number of calculations. .

As in the 486, Pentium processors use clock multipliers:

Processor Velocity	Motherboard Velocity (Bus speed)	Multiplier
Pentium 60 MHz	60 MHz	1x
Pentium 66 MHz	66 MHz	1x
Pentium 75 MHz	50 MHz	1,5 x
Pentium 90 MHz	60 MHz	1,5 x
Pentium 100 MHz	66 MHz	1,5 x
Pentium 120 MHz	60 MHz	2 x
Pentium 133 MHz	66 MHz	2 x
Pentium 150 MHz	60 MHz	2,5 x
Pentium 166 MHz	66 MHz	2,5 x
Pentium 180 MHz	60 MHz	3 x
Pentium 200 MHz	66 MHz	3 x

As at the time of the 486, motherboards for the Pentium (with the exception of some very old boards) support various bus frequencies and multipliers and may be configured to function with all processors in the family. You can almost always make an upgrade from a Pentium 100 to a Pentium 200 for example, simply by changing the processor and configuring the motherboard.

Another improvement in the Pentium, and one of the principal reasons for its superior performance is the adoption of a superscalar architecture. The Pentium is comprised of two distinct 32 bit processors internally, capable of executing two instructions per clock cycle (one in each processor). A control unit was included also that has the function of controlling the functions of each, and sharing the tasks between them.

As in fact the Pentium is a set of two 32 bit processors functioning in parallel, its is possible to access memory using binary words of 64 bits, double that of the 486, which accessed memory using 32 bits. This resource permits 8 bytes to be read in each cycle instead of only 4 doubling the access time and substantially reducing the old problem of slow memory access.

Due to this 64 bit memory access method, it is always necessary to use two 72 pin memory modules in pairs. Given that each module permits access using 32 bit words, we therefore access 64 bits when both are accessed simultaneously.

Even having the 64 bit memory access capacity, and having two internal processors of 32 bits, the Pentium continues being a 32 bit processor. These new resources served only to improve the performance of the processor.

Processors

AMD 5x86

This processor was launched by AMD shortly after the debut of the Pentium. In spite of the name, the 5x86 is really a 486 processor that functions at 133Mhz with a motherboard bus frequency of 33Mhz and a multiplier of 4x.

Cyrix Cx5x86

As well as designing 486 processors that were manufactured by Texas Instruments, Cyrix launched a processor that combined various features of the 486 and the Pentium, offering a performance well above a normal 486.

Like the AMDs 5x86, the Cx5x86 is 100% compatible with 486 motherboards, being sufficient to jumper the motherboard with a multiplier of 3x and a clock frequency of 33Mhz for the 100Mhz version, and 3x @ 40Mhz for the 120Mhz version

AMD K5

Instead of simply making a clone (a processor equal to Intel), AMD opted to develop a completely new processor, technically superior to the Pentium. The K5 also uses a superscalar architecture, but instead of two, there are four processors working in parallel. The L2 cache was also increased to 24Kb.

The math coprocessor however was not improved much, presenting an inferior performance to that of the Pentium coprocessor, turning its performance weak in graphical applications and games.

As in the majority of applications the K5 was much faster than the Pentium, AMD opted to market their processor according to a PR Index, that compared its performance to a Pentium.

Processor	Real operating frequency
K5-Pr 120	90 MHz (1,5x 60 MHz)
K5-Pr 133	100 MHz (1,5x 66 MHz)
K5-Pr 166	116 MHz (1,75x 66 MHz)

Pentium MMX

Launched at the beginning of 1997, the MMX is very similar to the original Pentium in architecture. However 57 new instructions were added to the microcode inside the processor that were aimed at improving its performance in multimedia applications and image processing. In these types of applications, some routines could be executed up to 400% faster with the use of MMX instructions. The performance gain is not automatic, however, so it is necessary to have software capable of taking advantage of these instructions, otherwise there is no gain at all.

It would be rather like living in a house and suddenly moving to another identical one but with one more door in the kitchen, hidden by a curtain, that led to other rooms. If nobody told you about the door you might be none the wiser and would continue to use the old rooms. An old program simply doesn't know of the existence of MMX instructions, and therefore has no performance gain whatsoever. In order to take advantage of the new instructions the programmer needs to alter his programs, changing the routines so that MMX instructions are used instead of the standard x86 ones The actual performance gain depends on the ability of the programmer to detect where MMX may be used to turn program execution faster.

The primary L1 processor cache was also increased in size to 32Kb making the MMX some 7% to 10% superior to the original Pentium even in instructions that do not use MMX. The Pentium MMX is found in 166, 200 and 233 MHz versions. The motherboard functions at 66 MHz in all of them (as in the normal Pentium).

Intel also launched MMX Overdrive processors, that could replace older 75, 100 or 120Mhz processors by a simple change of processor. The problem is that these processors are much more expensive and hard to find as well as not being very attractive. In terms of cost benefit ratio they are not a good option. In case your motherboard doesn't offer support for MMX processors it is as well to change this also.

With regard to support most people have many doubts about the installation of MMX in older motherboards. The MMX may not be used in many motherboards due to its dual voltage system. With the MMX the internal or "Core" components function at a voltage of 2.8V whilst the I/O circuits that connect the processor with the external world continue using a voltage of 3.3V as in the original Pentium. This dual system was created to reduce the heat generated by the processor. Many older motherboards are only capable of supplying 3.3V and 3.5V as used by the Pentium and VRE and for this reason are incompatible with the MMX.

Any motherboard that supports the Pentium could in theory support the MMX also, because the difference is only in the circuits voltage regulators that as well as the 3.3V and 3.5Vs, should also support dual –voltage of 2.8 to 3.3V. The MMX instructions are only software and do not require any type of support on behalf of the motherboard. For this reason all motherboards for the MMX also support the common Pentium, haking it necessary only to set the jumpers for the correct voltages.

AMD K6

As in the K5, the K6 is comprised internally of 4 distinct processors wich permits it to process more instructions simultaneously. The L1 cache was increased to 64KB also. The K6 also has the MMX instructions and maintains compatibility with motherboards for the Pentium MMX. Other resources found in the Pentium like the provision of dynamic deviation and speculative read-ahead are also used to improve the performance of the K6.

Because of its more advanced architecture the K6 exceeds not only the Pentium but also the Pentium MMX, reaching close to the Pentium II itself in some applications.

The Achilles heel of the K6, however, is its math coprocessor which has a much more simple architecture that that used by Intel in the Pentium MMX and Pentium II and for this reason it is much slower.

Although this defect does not affect the performance of the K6 in Office applications, in graphics applications, like image processing or video, 3 dimensional games (like Quake II) are sufficiently downgraded.In these applications the K6 may be up to 20% slower than a Pentium MMX with the same clock frequency.

AMD K6-2

Following the example of Intel, that added the MMX instructions to the standard instruction set, AMD incorporated 27 new instructions in the K6-2 processors. These instructions are called "3D-Now!" and have the objective of facilitating the processing of three- dimensional images, functioning in conjunction with a 3D accelerator video card. As happens with MMX, it is necessary to have software that makes use of 3D-Now!. Happily Microsoft included support to these new instructions of the K6-2 in their DirectX 6, in such a way that games and other applications may benefit indirectly from the new K6-2 instructions. Several game makers have also optimized their products for the new K6-2 instructions and even games not optimized may benefit from the new instructions with the help of new optimized video card drivers.

As well as the new instructions, the K6-2 processors work with a bus frequency of 110MHz and there are versions from 300Mhz upwards. Compatibility with MMX instructions was maintained

In spite of the K6-2 using motherboards with a bus frequency of 100Mhz, it may also be used in older motherboards that have a bus of only 66Mhz. In this case, a 300Mhz K6-2 may be used with a bus frequency of 66Mhz and a multiplier of 4.5x. Obviously , a little performance is lost in this way. The motherboard should also have support for the 2.2V used by the K6-2.

Cyrix 6x86MX

The 6x86MX is Cyrix's answer to Intel's MMX. Like the K6, the processor has an L1 cache of 64Kb and four internal processors. It also has MMX instructions and is compatible with the motherboards used by the MMX and K6.

Its performance in Windows applications is very similar to the K6, however the math co-processor is even slower than that of the K6, greatly reducing its performance in games and other floating point calculation intensive applications.

For office applications like Word processors etc. the 6x86 is a good option due to its low price, but is not adequate if the principal use of the micro is graphics programs or games.

Like the K5, the 6x86 adopted the PR Index. The 6x86MX may be found in the following versions. PR150 (120 MHz), PR166 (133 MHz), PR200 (166 MHz), PR233 (187 or 200 MHz depending on the series) and PR266 (225 or 233 MHz). The PR Index is only a comparative index, saying that in spite of a clock speed of only 233 MHz, the 6x86 PR266 has a performance 33% superior to that of a Pentium 200 MHz.

Recently, Cyrix also launched the 6x86MII processors, that are nothing more than a continuation of the 686MX series, but now with indices of PR 300, 333, 350 e 400.

Pentium Pro

Up to this point the processors have been presented more or less in chronological order, but there is an exception to this, the Pentium Pro. Actually, this processor was launched well before the MMX, being a contemporary of the original Pentium. However the architecture used in the Pentium Pro was used as a base for the Pentium II and the Pentium III as well as the Xeon and the Celeron.

The Pentium Pro was developed to compete in the high performance market, equipping workstations and servers. In spite of having some Pentium technology, the Pentium Pro was an almost completely new design., bringing radical architectural changes. Among the innovations brought by the Pentium Pro was the superscalar architecture with three channels (or in other words, three processors working in parallel, as opposed to two in the Pentium), multi-processing support, permitting the use of up to four Pentium Pro processors in the same motherboard working in parallel, and finally the L2 cache which stopped being a part of the motherboard and became integrated with the processor. In spite of everything, the Pentium Pro is still a 32 bit processor.

Because it uses a new type of encapsulation, the Pentium Pro uses a new type of socket, called socket 8, incompatible with the normal socket 7s. A new chipset, the i440FX, was created in order to permit the use of all the new resources brought by the Pentium Pro. The socket 8 is much larger than the socket 7 used by the original Pentium and similar processors, also having a different pin layout that only permits insertion the correct way. As the L2 cache is integrated with the processor, the motherboards don't have any cache at all.

The biggest problem with the Pentium Pro is its slowness in running 16 bit programs, like applications developed for MS-DOS and Windows 3.1 Windows 95/98 also falls into this category as it is actually a hybrid system, theoretically 32 bits, but also uses 16 bit instructions. When running these application, the Pentium Pro presents a performance very similar to the original Pentium in spite of all the improvements. It only shows its true potential when running full 32 bit operating systems, like Windows NT.

The Pentium Pro was produced in versions equipped with clock speeds of 166 and 200Mhz, and with L2 cache memories of 256, 512 or 1024 KB.

Pentium II

Intel developed the Pentium II using the Pentium Pro as a base. On the one hand, whilst some improvements were made, on the other, some resources were removed (like the support for four processors), leaving it more suited to the domestic market.

The most visible change in the Pentium II is the new processor format. From a small ceramic capsule, there was now a circuit board, which contained the processor and the integrated L2 cache. There is a small plastic box protecting this circuit board, forming a cartridge rather like a video game cartridge. The Pentium II also uses a new type of socket, called Slot One by Intel and requires an appropriate motherboard.

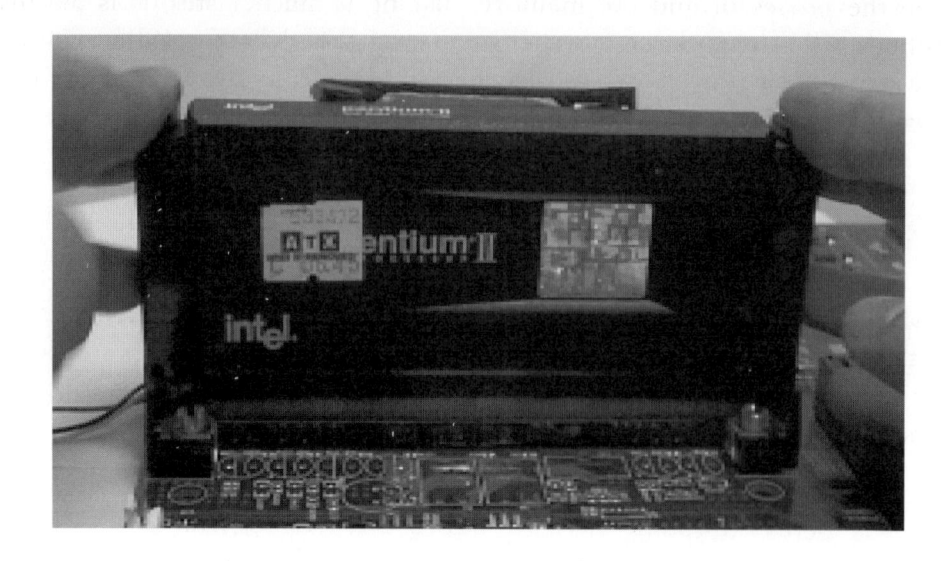

Pentium II being fitted in a motherboard

The Pentium II brings a 32Kb L2 cache, a 512Kb integrated L2 cache and compatibility with the MMX instructions. It also offers support for up to 4GB of RAM memory

As the Pentium II was developed for the home market, Intel soon found a way of solving the 16 bit problem of the Pentium Pro, through the addition of a segment register. A opposed to its predecessor, the Pentium II could process 16 bit instructions as fast as those of 32 bits, thus offering a good performance whether running DOS, Windows 3.1 or Windows 95/98.

INTEGRATED L2 CACHE

The Pentium II had no less than 512KB of L2 cache integrated with the processor, twice as much as found in the simpler versions of the Pentium Pro. However the cache in the Pentium II worked at only half of the processor clock speed. For example, in a 266Mhz Pentium II, the L2 cache worked at 133 MHz, double the speed of the cache used in socket 7 motherboards, (that function at the same speed as the motherboard) , but still much less than the 2000Mhz cache of the Pentium Pro. Intel chose to use this slower cache to reduce production costs of the processor.

You will never see a motherboard for the Pentium II with a cache, since that the cache is always integrated with the processor itself.

The last consideration in respect of Pentium II processors is the bus frequency, in other words the velocity of the mother board used by the processor. Versions of the Pentium II up to 333 MHz functioned using a clock speed of 66 MHz, whilst the versions from 350Mhz up function at 100 MHz, speeding up the exchange of data between the processor and the memory, making it much faster. It is worthwhile remembering that the newest motherboards, equipped with i440BX, i440GX or i440ZX chipsets support a bus frequency of 100 MHz. It is also necessary to use PC-100 memory, which will be explained in more details in the chapter on memory.

Celeron

With the launching of the Pentium II Intel abandoned manufacturing the Pentium MMX, selling only Pentium II processors which were much more expensive. The result of this strange strategy was the loss of almost all the low cost computer market, where the Pentium II was literally massacred by AMD's K6 and Cyrix's 6x86, which in spite of a markedly inferior performance, cost less than half the price of a Pentium II of the same clock speed.

Intel resolved to launch a low cost version of the Pentium II baptized Celeron (from the Latin "Celerus" tmeaning velocity) in order to try to repair the damage done. The Celeron is **identical** to the Pentium II, the only changes being the integrated L2 cache which is smaller in the Celeron and the absence of the plastic cover, the circuit board is esposed

Celeron

The first versions of the Celeron, which include all of the 266 and some of the 300 mhz models, did not have any L2 cache, and for this reason had a very weak performance in the majority of applications, in spite of still having a reasonable performance in games and other programs that depend on the math co-processor.

The L2 Cache is an extremely important component of today's processors because in spite of the processing power having increased more than 1000 times in the last two decades, RAM memory has not evolved very much in speed. It is no use having a super fast processor if it has to stop what it is doing every instant to wait for data to come from RAM memory. It is there that the secondary cache comes into play, reuniting the most important data from memory so that the processor is not kept waiting. By removing the L2 cache, the performance of the equipment fell almost 40%, and was only not worse because the Lq cache was still being used. For this reason as well as losing badly to its older brother, the no-cache Celeron lost even to less advanced processors, like the MMX, the K6 and the 6x86MX.In fact a 266Mhz Celeron without a cache even lost to a 233MMX in some applications.

The Celeron without a cache was not well received on the market due to its low performance. Because of this Intel decided to equip the newer versions of the Celeron with a 128KB L2 cache which, unlike the the Pentium II's cache , functioned at the same speed as the processor. **All Celerons on sale nowadays have a cache**, including all versions of 333Mhz and above and the majority of those of 300Mhz. Those of 300Mhz with a cache are called 300A to differentiate them from those without a cache.

This 128K cache made an incredible difference in processor performance. While an older Celeron is almost 40% slower than a Pentium II with the same clock speed, the Celeron with a cache is only about 5% slower, equaling it in some applications. This happens because even though the Celeron has four times less cache, it functions twice as fast, thus compensating for the difference.

A Celeron costs approximately half the price of Pentium II with the same clock speed, being an option with a greater cost-benefit ratio, considering that it has almost the same performance.

The cached Celeron is being produced in versions that go from 300 to 500Mhz, all with a bus frequency of 66Mhz.

Socket 370 vs Slot One

Initially Intel launched the Celeron A in the same format as the Pentium II, that is in the form of a circuit board that fitted into a Slot One. Soon afterwards they began to produce the Celeron using a new type of encapsulation PPGA (Plastic Pin Grid Array), that fitted into a Socket 370.

The format is very similar to a MMX. The difference is that the Celeron has quite a few more pins:

The socket 370 uses the same pin numbers as a Slot One and the motherboards use the same chipsets and other basic components. It is even possible to fit a socket 370 Celeron in a Slot One motherboard with the help of an adapter that costs about $15 (nicknamed Sloket). The processor is socketted in the adapter that in turn is slotted into the motherboard as shown below:

Intel's excuse for suddenly changing the format of the Celeron was that after the L2 cache was moved inside the processor encapsulation the circuit board used in the Pentium II was no longer necessary, serving only to increase production costs. By removing it, it was possible to produce processors with a lower cost.

The Celeron is still being made at the moment in the two formats, both for socket 370 and the PPGA for Slot One (that are slightly more expensive), although the performance of each one is identical.

Pentium II Xeon

The Xeon uses basically the same architecture as the Pentium II, the only difference being the L2 cache that functions at the same speed as the processor in the Xeon (as happens in the Celeron and the Pentium Pro). The Pentium II Xeon is sold in versions with a cache of 512, 1024 and 2048 KB and in velocities of 400, 450 and 500 MHz.

The Xeon was designed especially to equip servers, replacing the Pentium Pro, as in these environments the processing is extremely repetitive, and makes a big difference with a bigger and faster but it does not make much sense to buy for domestic use in view of its high price. Another important resource of the Xeon is the possibility of using up to 4 processors in the same motherboard without any additional hardware and up to 8 in case the motherboard has a special circuit called a cluster . (The Pentium II only permits the use of two processors). Obviously a special motherboard is needed to use more than one processor.

Pentium III

Contrary to what it's name suggests , the Pentium III is only a faster Pentium II. The architecture is exactly the same, with the integrated L2 cache the same at 512Kb operating at half the processor speed and using the same packaging.

As both processors are compatible, motherboards developed for the Pentium III support both the Pentium II and the Celeron. The majority of mother boards with a bus frequency of 100Mhz produced for the Pentium II as from the beginning of 1999 may be used with a Pentium II without any problems.

The only improvement was the addition of new instructions called SSE to the processor. These new instructions are similar to those of the K6-2's 3D-Now! As used in the K6-2 they are capable of improving the processor performance in floating point applications. As always, in order to realize this performance gain, software needs to be rewritten to take advantage of the new instructions.

As the SSE instructions only give a performance gain in mathematical calculations, only games, image or video editing and other calculation intensive applications gain any benefit. The creators of Quake 3 Arena, a game optimized for the new instructions estimate that the performance gain using a Pentium III is approximately 20 to 30% because of the new instructions. Adobe Photoshop 5.02, that was also optimized for the new instructions has a gain in performance of around 20%.

Together with the Pentium III, Intel also launched the Pentium III Xeon that is nothing more than a Pentium II Xeon with the new SSE instruction set.

AMD K6-3

The K6-3, launched a little before the Pentium III is a specially muscular version of the K6-2. The processors appear much the same, same architecture, same math co-processor and the same 3D-Now! instructions. What changed was the L2 cache.

Whilst in the K6 and K6-2, the L2 cache is part of the motherboard and functions at the same frequency (66 or 100Mhz), in the K6-3 the L2 cache was moved inside the processor. There is a total L2 cache of 25KB but functioning at the same frequency as the processor, which makes the K6-3 cache more efficient than the Pentium II's cache.

The K6-3 continues being compatible with the socket 7 motherboards as used in the K6-2. Any motherboard that supports the AMD K6-2 at 400 MHz, will also support the K6-3 of 400 and 450 MHz without any problems. The same voltage, 2.2V, is used by both the K6-2 and the K6-3, therefore dispensing with any additional configuration. In case the motherboard has a cache, this is automatically used as an L3 cache again dispensing with any additional configuration.

The faster cache significantly increased the performance of the K6-3 in relation to the K6-2. In office type applications a K6-3 of 450 MHz may be superior to a Pentium III of 500 MHz, however in games and graphics applications it can be 20% slower than a Pentium III with the same frequency.

AMD Athlon (K7)

Since the K5, AMD processors have always lost to Intel in terms of performance of the math co-processor, being a good option for those who work with Office applications but offering a weak performance in graphics applications. AMD opted to design a completely new processor initially baptized the Athlon to solve this problem. As expected, it was named the K7.

The Athlon brings with it no less than 128 KB of L1 cache, double that of the K6-2 and K6-3, and four times that of the Pentium II and Pentium III. The L2 cache L2 is integrated with the processors the first versions having 512 KB. AMD have promised to launch Athlon versions with up to 8 MB of L2 cache in the near future.

The math co-processor was completely redesigned and now is composed of nothing less than 3 co-processors working in parallel. The processor nucleus was also improved and now processes instructions in 9 stages (The Pentium III processes instructions in 5 stages).

The Athlon is a processor technically superior to the Pentium III, being considered a seventh generation processor (The Pentium III is still considered a sixth generation processor). This superiority is reflected in the performance: The Athlon manages to be superior both in Office applications as well as in graphics applications. A 500Mhz

HARDWARE PC

Athlon easily beats a 550Mhz Pentium III in the majority of applications.

All this sophistication however, made the Athlon incompatible with the socket 7 motherboards used in conjunction with the K6-2 and K6-3. In order to use it a specially constructed motherboard will be needed. There are already some models on the market that have a price well above those of Pentium III motherboards. Other readily available components on the market (memory, hard disks, video cards, etc.) continue to be compatible with the Athlon.

PERFORMANCE COMPARISONS

Now that you know each processor's resources and capacities, nothing better than to see how fast each one is in practice. Following are two graphs which show the performance of the processors in office type applications and in graphics applications. These graphs also will help at the time of deciding which processor is best to buy, taking into account both the price and the applications for which the micro is destined.

Integer performance

As we have already seen, the performance of the processor in whole number processing determines its performance only in Office type applications. The results of the test were obtained using Business Winstone 98, considered one of the most accurate performance indicators available at the moment:

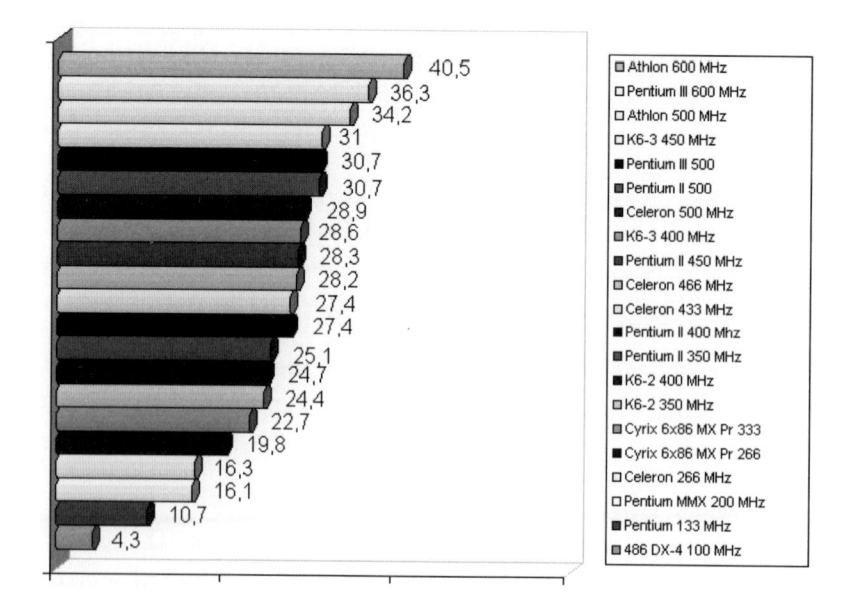

Processor	Score
Athlon 600 MHz	40,5
Pentium III 600 MHz	36,3
Athlon 500 MHz	34,2
K6-3 450 MHz	31
Pentium III 500	30,7
Pentium II 500	30,7
Celeron 500 MHz	28,9
K6-3 400 MHz	28,6
Pentium II 450 MHz	28,3
Celeron 466 MHz	28,2
Celeron 433 MHz	27,4
Pentium II 400 Mhz	27,4
Pentium II 350 MHz	25,1
K6-2 400 MHz	24,7
K6-2 350 MHz	24,4
Cyrix 6x86 MX Pr 333	22,7
Cyrix 6x86 MX Pr 266	19,8
Celeron 266 MHz	16,3
Pentium MMX 200 MHz	16,1
Pentium 133 MHz	10,7
486 DX-4 100 MHz	4,3

FPU Performance

The term FPU (floating point unit) is used in comparative benchmarks to indicate the performance of the processor when dealing with fractional numbers and complex or floating point operations. Other following graph results were obtained using 3D Winbench 99, one of the most accurate tests used at the moment for measuring the FPU performance:

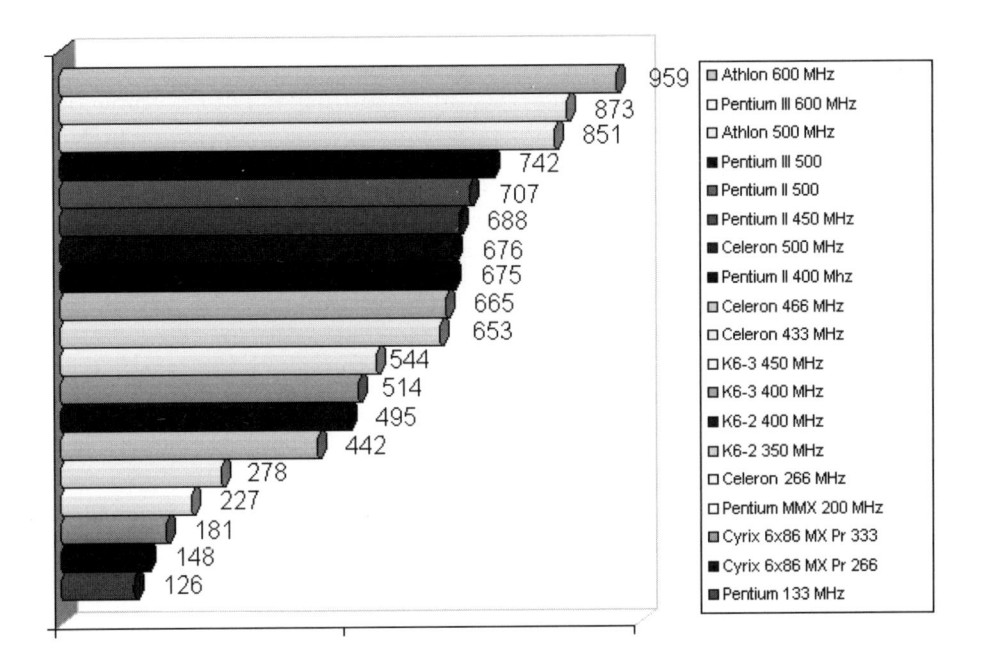

Processor	Score
Athlon 600 MHz	959
Pentium III 600 MHz	873
Athlon 500 MHz	851
Pentium III 500	742
Pentium II 500	707
Pentium II 450 MHz	688
Celeron 500 MHz	676
Pentium II 400 Mhz	675
Celeron 466 MHz	665
Celeron 433 MHz	653
K6-3 450 MHz	544
K6-3 400 MHz	514
K6-2 400 MHz	495
K6-2 350 MHz	442
Celeron 266 MHz	278
Pentium MMX 200 MHz	227
Cyrix 6x86 MX Pr 333	181
Cyrix 6x86 MX Pr 266	148
Pentium 133 MHz	126

3 RAM Memory

RAM memory is one of the most essential components of a PC. It is impossible for a computer to work without at least a minimum quantity of RAM memory, because the processor needs this memory to store programs and data that are being used.

In days gone by RAM memory was very expensive. Until just a few years ago the cost was about $40 per megabyte. Because of this high cost, many computers came equipped with only 8MB or even sometimes 4MB even though the minimum recommended for graphical systems like Windows is at least 16MB. Happily the price has fallen drastically in the last few years and memory such as SDRAM can now be found for about $1.50 per megabyte.

The low price nowadays justifies the use of 64MB or even 128MB of memory. The quantity and speed of memory are more important than the processor speed, especially for those who work with Office applications, images or are accustomed to work with several applications open at the same time.

When there is insufficient memory installed, Windows uses the hard disk to simulate the existence of more memory, thus permitting programs to execute even when all the physical memory is totally used up. This concept is called **virtual memory**, and consists of creating a temporary file on the hard disk called a **swap file**, saving the data that doesn't fit into memory in this. The problem is that when the programs run, everything becomes extremely slow because the hard disk is thousands of times slower than RAM memory. The more data that needs to be saved in the swap file, the worse the performance becomes. It is no use having an extremely fast processor because if there is little memory available its performance is limited to the speed of the hard disk and under utilized due to the use of virtual memory.

Just to have an idea of how important the quantity of RAM memory is, a simple 486 with a reasonable quantity of RAM memory, say 32MB or more, is capable of running Windows 95/98 and the majority of applications much more rapidly than a Pentium III 500 with only 8MB of memory. Which do you think is faster, a 486 processor, or the hard disk used in a Pentium III?

Obviously the ideal is to have a balanced system, it would be a waste of time to put 64MB of RAM memory in a 386.

FORMAT

Memory chips are fragile pieces of silicon that need to be encapsulated in some more resistant type of structure before being transported and installed in the motherboard. Just as there are various types of packaging for different processors, (for example SEC and PPGA) memory cards come packaged in different ways. Initially the chips are encapsulated in plastic modules called DIP that protects them and helps to dissipate the heat generated by the chips. These in turn are soldered onto little printed circuit boards thus forming memory modules. There are 3 main type of memory modules, 30 pin SIMM, 72 pin SIMM and finally the newest, 168 pin DIMM.

30 pin simm memory modules

The first memory modules to be manufactured were called an acronym for "Single In Line Memory Module" because there are only contacts for the pins on one side. Although there are contacts on the reverse side as well, they are only an extension of the front contacts serving to increase the contact area in the motherboard socket. If you examine the contacts closely you will see a very small hole in each that serves to join the two sides.

The first SIMM memory modules had 30 pins and were capable of working with data transfer of 8 bits at a time. These modules were used in 386 and 486 micros and were manufactured in several capacities, the most common being 1MB and 4MB, although there are also 512Kb, 8MB and 16MB modules.

30 pin SIMM memory module

As both the 386 and the 486 are processors that access memory using 32 bit words, 4 modules need to be used to form one memory bank, that is to say, as the processor needed 32 bits and each module could only supply 8, then the 4 modules together could supply the necessary 32 bits as if it was one complete 32 bit word. Therefore, these memory modules must always be used in groups of 4 or a multiple thereof.

In computers equipped with the 386SX only 2 modules are necessary, seeing that the 386SX accesses memory using words of only 16 bits.

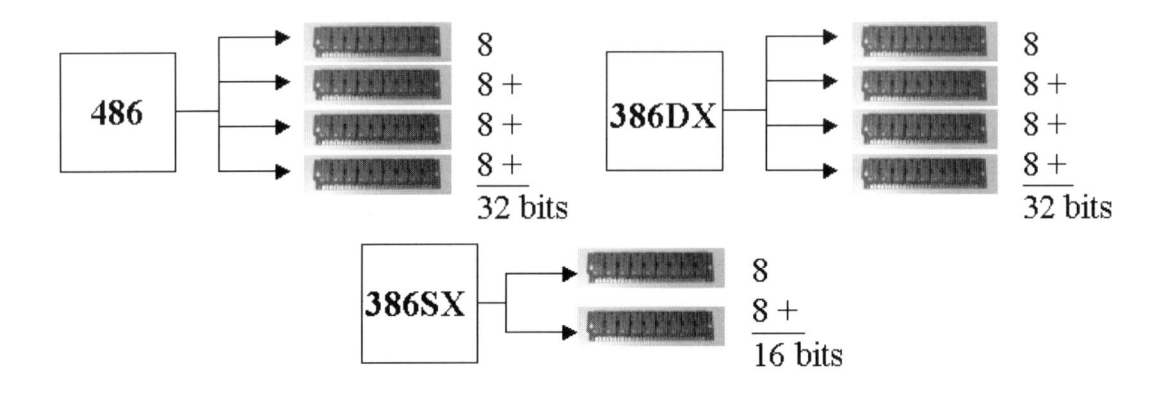

```
                                8                                    8
                                8 +                                  8 +
    486                         8 +          386DX                   8 +
                                8 +                                  8 +
                                ────                                 ────
                                32 bits                              32 bits

                                            8
                      386SX                 8 +
                                            ────
                                            16 bits
```

It is important to remember that the 4 modules which form one bank should be identical, otherwise the computer could lock up. You may use 4 modules of one type in one bank and 4 modules of a different type in another bank, but you can never mix different types in one bank.

72 pin memory modules

In spite of being much more practical than the DIP chips, 30 pin SIMM modules were still very inconvenient, especially as 4 identical modules were needed to make up one memory bank. The manufacturers created a new type of memory module, called SIMM which used 32 bits and with 72 pins to get around this problem. This kind of memory was used in the later 486s and became standard in the Pentiums.

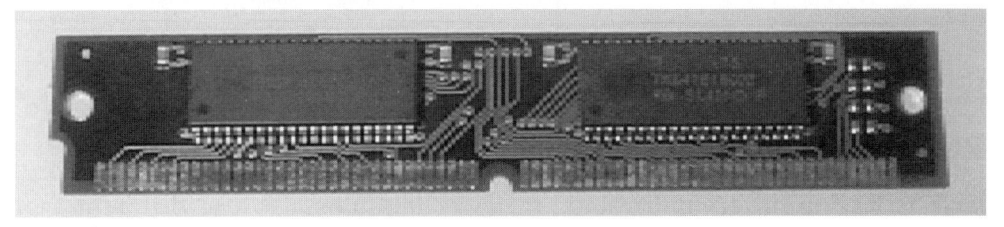

72 pin SIMM memory module

Instead of 4 modules, only one 72 pin SIMM was needed to form each memory bank in the 486s, thus permitting the use of any combination and quantity of

36 HARDWARE PC

SIMMs as each alone formed a memory bank. As the Pentium accessed memory using 64 bit words, 2 memory modules were necessary to form each bank, which is why there are always two pairs in the Pentium. If you want to install 16MB of memory, you need two modules each of 8MB, or 4 modules of 4MB, you can never install a single module of 16MB as was done in the 486.

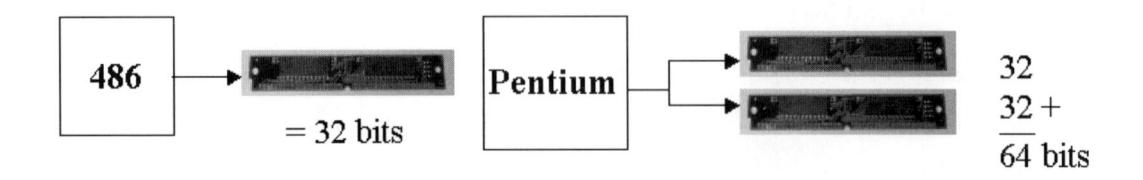

168 pin DIMM memory

Unlike the 30 pin and 72 pin SIMM modules, the DIMM modules have contacts on both sides of the circuit board that gives rise to its name, "Double In Line Memory Module". A single module is sufficient to complete a memory bank as DIMM memory modules work with 64 bit binary words, and it is not necessary to use them in pairs. For example if you want to install 64MB in a Pentium you only need to buy a single module of 64MB.

Nowadays 168 DIMM memories are the only type manufactured. It is difficult to find 72 pin memories, or even motherboards that support them anymore.

168 PIN DIMM MEMORY MODULE

TYPES OF TECHNOLOGY USED

As well as having different formats, memory modules also use different type of technology. There are FPM, EDO e SDRAM (that is sub-divided into SDRAM PC-100 and PC-66) memories.

FPM (Fast Page Mode) Memory

FPM memory is the oldest type of memory that can still be found today. Even though it is still to be found in modern computers, this type is n longer used because it is very slow when compared to EDO and SDRAM.

This kind of memory can be found in both 30 pin and 72 pin memory modules and almost always has an access time of 70 or 80 nanoseconds.

Edo (Extended Data Output) Memory

Even though already outdated, this kind of memory is still much used at the moment, manufactured in speeds of 50, 60, and 70 nano seconds, 60 nano seconds being the most common. The difference between FPM memory and EDO is that EDO has several improvements in its architecture which make it about 20% faster.

EDO memory is to be found in the 72 pin format, although there have been some manufactured in modules with 168 pins, but these are very rare.

All 30 pin memory modules are FPM, while (excepting some very old modules) and 168 pin memory modules are SDRAM.

Confusion only exists in modules with 72 pins, that may be either FPM or EDO memory. In order to know which is which, you only have to look at the access time. Every memory module has its data stamped on the chips in the form of a code, the access time is indicated at the end of the first line. If this finishes with –7, -70, or only 7, or 70, the module has an access time of 70 nano seconds. If the line finishes with –6, -60, 6 or 60 the access time is 60 nano seconds.

As almost all modules with an access time of 70 nano seconds are FPM and almost all EDO memories have an access time of 60 nano seconds, you can be certain of using this method to determine what kind of memory it is.

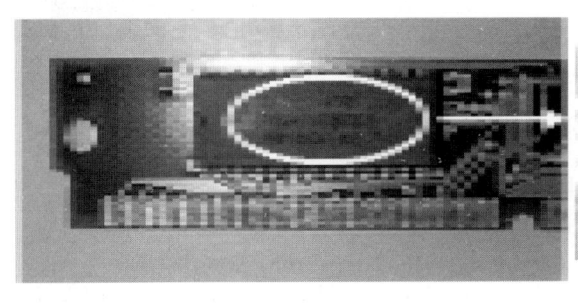

SDRAM (Synchronous Dynamic RAM) Memory

All memory whether FPM or EDO are asynchronous which means they were at their own rhythm, independent of the motherboard clock. This explains why memory FPM, designed to be used in a 386 or 486 (that worked at 25 or 33Mhz), may be used in Pentium motherboards that function at 66Mhz. Actually the memory keeps functioning at the same frequency, but what changes are the waiting times wich become higher. Instead of responding to the processor each 3 cycles of the motherboard clock, they may end up responding only every 6 cycles, although functioning normally.

SDRAM memory however is capable of working synchronized with the motherboard cycles without any wait states. This means that the timing of memory SDRAM is always one read per cycle, independent of the motherboard speed.

As the SDRAM memory that you want to use needs to be at least fast enough to keep up with the motherboard to be used, you will find memories with access times between 6 and 15 nano seconds. To know the access time of a module you just have to look at the end of the first line of codes that will finish with −15, -12, -10, -9, -8, -7 or -6, indicating that the module has (respectively) access times of 15, 12, 10, 9, 8, 7 or nano seconds.

To determine the maximum operating frequency of SDRAM all you have to do is divide 1000 by its access time. A SDRAM with an access time of 15 nano seconds may function at a maximum frequency of MHz, i.e. 1000/15 = 66. Another with an access time of 12 nano seconds may function at 75 or even 83 MHz, given that 1000/12 = 83. To check the validity of this calculation all you have to is divide 1 second by 83,000,000 clock cycles of the motherboard and you will get 12 nano seconds.

It is worthwhile to remember that these values are only theoretical, a normal SDRAM memory with an access time of, for example, 10 nano seconds is not guaranteed to work in a motherboard that operates at 100Mhz, as used by Pentium II processors (above 350Mhz)), K6-2, Pentium III etc, because it was designed and guaranteed to function at 66 MHz only.

PC-100 (100Mhz memory) Memory

The PC-100 standard, developed by IBM, consists of a series of specifications that are aimed at making memories that can function with stability in motherboards that operate at 100 MHz. Theoretically, any SDRAM memory with an access time of 10ns or less may function at 100 MHz, because 1000/10 = 100. The problem is that although some SDRAM modules (called PC-66 because they are guaranteed for a frequency of 66Mhz only) offer access times of 10ns or even 9ns, they often have a very high latency time and can't keep up when they have to work at 100

MHz.

Although the manufacturers initially had problems making PC-100 memories, with the proliferation of processors that operate with a BUS of 100 MHz, such as the Pentium II in the 350, 400, 450 and 500 MHz versions and K6s of 300, 350, 400 and 450 MHz, these memories have become very popular. Memories PC-100 with access times of 10, 9, 8, 7 or even 6ns may be found on sale at the moment.

It is worth remembering that good even quality SDRAM memories may function at 100 Hz, but that there is not any type of guarantee, it is rather like a shot in the dark. As well as this, SDRAM memories working at this velocity are not quite as dependable.

Normally PC-100 memory comes with a label on which is printed "PC-100" or "100", obviously this is not any guarantee because the label may have been put there by an unscrupulous vendor. Unhappily there is no way to be certain even by examining the module visually only by testing it, which is not always possible. But you don't need to worry too much because practically all memory manufactured nowadays is PC-100. The possibility of acquiring PC-66 is more evident only if you are buying used memory modules.

ECC AND PARITY

No matter how good the quality, all types of memory may have errors which can be caused by innumerous factors, that may go from momentary interference to actual physical defects in the memory. Although errors in memory modules are quite rare, if data is altered it might cause a lot of collateral effects. To increase the grade of reliability of systems, methods were created to diagnose and correct errors.

An error correction system is not so important in a domestic computer because at worst an error in memory (which is rare) would cause the computer to lock up. In critical applications however such as a bank, any processing error could cause large losses.

Nowadays the two main methods used for detection of errors in memory are **Parity** and **ECC** ("Error-Correcting Code"), based on totally different techniques:

The **Parity** is an older method, that is only capable of recognizing alterations in the data contained in memory and is not able to make any type of correction. Parity consists in the addition of one more bit for each byte of memory, thus each byte has 9 bits, the last one having the function of diagnosing alterations in the data.

The data verifying operation in the parity system is very simple: The number of "1" bits is counted in each byte. If the number is even, the parity bit is set to "1" and in case it is not an even number the 9th bit is set to a value of "0". When requested by the processor, the data is checked by the parity checking circuits that verify if the number of "1" bits corresponds to the value of the 9th bit. In case the data has been altered it sends an error message to the processor.

It is clear that this method is not 100% efficient, because it is not capable of detecting a change in the number of bits that result in no change in the parity. In case, for example, of two zero bits being altered to ones, the parity circuit would not note any alteration in the data. Luckily the possibility of two or more bits being altered at the same time is remote.

Processor	Real operating frequency
K5-Pr 120	90 MHz (1,5x 60 MHz)
K5-Pr 133	100 MHz (1,5x 66 MHz)
K5-Pr 166	116 MHz (1,75x 66 MHz)

The circuits responsible for data checking are independent from the rest of the system. Its only side effect is to make memory more expensive, because each byte has 9 bits instead of 8 bits, making it about 12% more expensive.

Previously memory was not manufactured without parity. As EDO e SDRAM memory of today presented a high level of reliability, the use of parity gradually was dispensed with. In fact there are few manufacturers who still produce memory with the 9th bit.

The ECC system was developed for systems destined to critical operations, a much more efficient diagnostic system, because as well as being capable of identifying data errors it can correct them through special algorithms. 1, 2 or even 3 extra bits may be found in a byte of ECC memory. The more bits destined to ECC, the more complex will be the codes stored and the chance of eventual errors being corrected will be greater.

In spite of not being very common in RAM memory, due to the high grade of reliability of these, ECC is an obligatory item in hard disks and CD-ROMs, because data corruption in these is much more common.

4   Hard Disks

The "Hard Disk", or "HD" as it is commonly referred to is a high capacity storage system that unlike the RAM memory, doesn't lose its data when the computer is switched off and therefore is used for long term or more permanent storage of data.

Although it is a magnetic media, an HD is very different from a normal diskette as it is composed of several platters that are mounted within a sealed unit because as the disks rotate at very high speed, any particle of dust, however small, that gets between the read heads and the disks would cause the disk surface to be scratched and render the unit unusable.

Without a doubt the hard disk is one of the components that has evolved the most in the history of computation. The first hard disk was constructed in 1957 by IBM and had no less than 50 platters with a diameter of 24 inches and a capacity of 5Mb, which was something quite incredible at that time.

This first hard disk was called a "Winchester" a term still used today to designate HDs of any kind. Up to the beginning of the 1980's hard disks were very expensive and 10MB models cost $2000, whilst today a 10Mb hard disk costs less than $200.

HOW THE HARD DISK FUNCTIONS

Data is recorded on magnetic disks within a hard disk called platters. These internal disks are comprised of two layers.

The first, called the substrate is nothing more than a metallic disk generally made of aluminum. In order to permit the storage of data this disk is covered with a second layer of magnetic material. The disks are mounted on a spindle which is rotated by a special motor.

To read and write data to the disk, reading heads are used which are fixed to a moveable arm that permits access to the whole disk. A special device called an actuator co-ordinates the movement of the read heads.

Diagram labels: Actuator, read arms, read and write heads, spindle, platters

HOW DATA IS WRITTEN AND READ

The magnetic disks of a hard disk are covered with an extremely fine magnetic layer. Actually, the finer the layer the more sensitive it becomes, and consequently the recording density will be more. Then we can store more data in a disk of the same size, thereby creating disks of greater capacity.

The first hard disks like those used in the beginning of the 1980s used the same magnetic media technology as used in diskettes, called "coated media", which as well as only allowing a low recording density were not very durable. The disks used nowadays use a laminated media (plated media); that is a denser media, with a much superior quality that in turn permits the enormous storage capacity of today's disks.

The read and write heads of a hard disk function as an electromagnet similar to what we studied in our first science lessons, being composed of an iron core with a coil of fine wire wound around it. The difference is that in a hard disk this electromagnet is extremely small and precise, such that it is capable of recording tracks measuring less than one hundredth of a millimeter.

When data is being recorded to the disk, the heads use their magnetic field to organize the iron oxide molecules on the recording surface with the positive poles of the molecules being lined up with the negative poles of the heads and their complement, the negative poles of the molecules aligned with the positive poles of the heads. This is the old law of "Opposites attract".

As the read and write heads of an HD are electromagnets, their polarity may be constantly alternated. With the disk spinning constantly by varying the polarity of the recording head we also vary the direction of the positive and negative poles of the magnetic surface. Depending on the direction of the poles we have our 0 or 1 bits.

To Record sequences of 0 and 1 bits that will form the data, the polarity of the magnetic heads is changed millions of times per second, but always following a clearly defined cycle. Each bit is formed on the disks by a sequence of several molecules. When the density of the disk is greater, less molecules may be used to store each bit and there is a weaker magnetic signal. Then a magnetic head with greater precision is needed.

When it is necessary to read the recorded data, the read head captures the magnetic field generated by the aligned molecules. The variation between the positive and negative magnetic signals generates a small electric current that flows in the coil. When this signal reaches the logic card of the HD it is interpreted as a sequence of 0 and 1 bits.

Looked at in this way it seems that the process of storing data in magnetic disks is simple and it really was in the first hard disks (like IBM's "Winchester"), that were constructed in an almost artisan manner. Although various improvements have been incorporated in modern disks, the basic process remains the same.

FORMATTING

In order that the operating system is capable of reading and writing data to the hard disk, it is first necessary to create structures that permit the data to be recorded in an organized manner, so that they can also be read back again later. This process is called **formatting**.

There are two types of format called **physical format and logical format**. Physical formatting is done only in the factory and consists of dividing the blank disk into tracks, sectors and cylinders. These demarcations function like the lanes on a highway, permitting the read head to know in what part of the disk it is and where it should record data. Physical formatting is done once only and may not be undone or redone by means of software.

However, in order that the disks can be recognized by the operating system, another type of format called logical format needs to be done. To the contrary of a physical format, a logical format does not alter the physical structure of the disk, and may be done and undone as often as you want, for example using DOS's **FORMAT** command. The format process is almost automatic, all you have to do is to execute the format program that comes together with the operating system. Later on there will be a whole chapter dedicated to explaining the format process using the programs FDISK and FORMAT of Windows.

When a disk is formatted its is simply organized in the way suitable to the operating system ready to receive data. This organization is called the filing system. A filing system is a set of logical structures and methods that permit the operating system to access the hard disk consistantly. Different operating systems use different filing systems.

The most common filing systems used at the moment are the **FAT16**, compatible with DOS and all versions of Windows and **FAT32**, compatible only with Windows 98 and Windows 95 OSR/2 (a debugged version of Windows 95), together with some improvements, sold only by Microsoft in new computers. Only these two will be explained because they are the systems used by Windows and consequently the majority of users. Other operating systems use their own proprietary filing systems, Windows NT and W2000 use NTFS whilst Linux uses EXT2

FAT 16

This is the filing system used by MS-DOS, including DOS 7.0, and by Windows 95, being compatible also with Windows 98 and Windows NT/2000. This filing system uses 16 bits for data addressing permitting a maximum of 65526 clusters, that may not be greater than 32 Kb. This is the biggest limitation of FAT16: as we can only have 65 thousand clusters with a maximum size of 32 KB each, the biggest partitions that can be created using this filing system are 2 Gigabytes. In case we have a bigger HD, it is necessary to divide it into two or more partitions. The operating system recognizes each partition as a separate disk: In case we have two partitions for example, the first would appear as C:\ and the second as D:\, exactly as if we had two hard disks installed in the computer

A cluster is the smallest allocation unit (the smallest unit of data that can be written at one time by the HD) recognized by the operating system., the FAT 16 has a limit of only 65 thousand clusters per partition (2 to the 16th power is 65,000). This limit exists because each cluster has to have a unique address through which it is possible to find where a specific file is stored. A large file is written to the disk fragmented over several clusters, but one cluster may not contain more than one file.

Each cluster has 32Kbytes in a 2Gb hard disk formatted with FAT16. Lets say that we wanted to write 10,000 text files to this disk, each one with only 300 bytes. As a cluster cannot contain more than one file, each file will use a whole cluster, that is 32Kbytes to Record 300 bytes! In total, these 10,000 files of 300 bytes each, instead of occupying only 3 Megabytes, will use up a total of 320 Megabytes on the disk! This is an enormous waste of space.

It is possible to use smaller clusters using FAT16, however in smaller partitions:

Partition Size	Cluster Size
Between 1 and 2 GB	32 Kbytes
Less than 1 GB	16 Kbytes
Less than 512 Mb	8 Kbytes
Less than 256 Mb	4 Kbytes
Less than 128 Mb	2 Kbytes

Due to the size of the clusters, it as not recommended to use FAT16 to format partitions with more than 1GB, with clusters of 32KB, the waste of disk space is excessive.

Windows 95 OSR/2 (also known as Windows "B") brought a new filing system called FAT FAT32 which also continues being used in Windows 98.

FAT 32

A natural evolution of the old FAT16, FAT32 uses 28 bits to address each cluster (in spite of, as the name suggests, 32 bits), permitting clusters of only 4 KB, even in partitions greater than 2GB. The maximum size of a partition with FAT32 is 2048 Gigabytes (2 Terabytes), that is adequate for the large capacity disk drives that are available at the moment.

Using this filing system, our 10,000 text files would occupy only 40Mb, a considerable saving in disk space. In fact, when a FAT16 partition is converted to FAT32 a reduction of occupied disk space in the order of 15% to 30% is normal. The problem is that other operating systems, including Linux, the older Windows 95, and OS/2 are not capable of accessing partitions formatted with FAT32; only Windows 95 OSR/2 and Windows 98 can do this. Windows NT 4.0 may be turned compatible with the help of third party programs, but FAT32 is not inherent in Windows NT.

Another problem is that due to the greater quantity of clusters to be managed, the performance of the HD falls slightly, approximately 3% to 5%, which in practice is imperceptible. Even so, if your only operating system is Windows 95 OSR/2 or Windows 98, the use of FAT32 is recommended due to it's support for large capacity disks and the savings in space.

LOGICAL STRUCTURES

A few pages ago, I said that logical formatting consisted in recording some structures on the disk, now let us see what these are.

Boot sector

When the computer is switched on, the BIOS (a small program recorded permanently in a chip on the motherboard, that has the function of kick starting the micro into action), will try to load the operating system. Independently of which filing system you are using, the first sector of the hard disk is reserved to store information about where to find the operating system, that permits BIOS to find it and start loading it.

What operating system is installed, with which filing system the hard disk is formatted and which files should be read to start loading the operating system is all recorded in the boot sector. A sector is the smallest physical division of a disk and always has 512 bytes. A cluster is the smallest part recognized by the operating system and may be composed of several sectors.

A single sector of 512 bytes may seem very little, but it is sufficient to store the boot Record due to its small size. The boot sector is also known as the MBR, track 0 etc.

FAT (File Allocation Table)

After a hard disk is formatted and divided into clusters, some more sectors are reserved for the FAT ("file allocation table". The function of the FAT is to serve as an index, storing information about each cluster on the disk. It is through the FAT that the operating system knows if a certain area of the disk is occupied or available and may find any stored.

Every time a new file is written or erased, the operating system alters the FAT, always maintaining it up to date. The FAT is so important, that because it is the main table a second copy is kept as a backup, that can always be used if the main table is damaged in some way.

It is curious to note that when we format a hard disk, using, for example, the **FORMAT** command, no data is erased, only the main FAT table is replaced by an empty table. Until the data is overwritten, it remains there, except that it is inaccessible.

Root directory

If we were to compare a hard disk with a book, the pages would be clusters, the FAT would serve as page numbers and cross references, while the root directory would be the index, with the name of each chapter and on what page it begins.

The root directory occupies some more sectors on the disk soon after the sectors occupied by the FAT. Each file or directory on the hard disk has an entry in the root directory, with the file name, it's extension, the date created or last modified, the size in bytes, and the cluster where each begins.

A small file may be stored in a single cluster, whilst a larger file is broken up and may occupy several clusters. In this case at the end of each cluster there will be a pointer to the next cluster occupied by the file. In the last occupied cluster there is an end of file marker

When a file is deleted, its entry in the root directory is simply removed making the clusters it used appear empty to the operating system. When it is necessary to record more data, these are simply recorded above the others, just as a cassette is rerecorded with other music.

RECOVERING DATA

Pay attention to the following paragraphs, because they will probably save your skin one day. :-)

The way in which data is recorded on the disk means that practically any erased data may be recovered. In fact, when a file is erased, whether through DOS or Windows Explorer only the reference to it in the FAT is erased. As the address previously occupied by the file is marked as vacant in the FAT, the operating system considers that the space occupied is vacant. However, nothing is really erased until new data is written over the old.

It is like rerecording on part of a cassette, the rest of the old music stays there.

Norton Utilities has a utility called "Rescue Disk" that permits storing a copy of the FAT on diskettes. In case your HD is accidentally formatted, whether by a virus or any other reason, you may restore the FAT with the help of these disks, returning to have access to all your data as if nothing had happened. Even if you don't have a copy of the FAT, there is another Norton Utilities program called Diskedit, that permits direct access to the disk clusters and (with some work) recover important data.

Another very interesting program to recover erased data is Tiramissu from Ontrack (www.ontrack.com), impressive by it's efficiency, even if there is not a copy of the FAT.

In spite of being small (the FAT32 version is only 450 Kb) Tiramissu is capable of recovering erased files or even a whole HD that has been erased by a virus, or when there is no vestige of the FAT left. It uses statistical probability techniques to attempt to guess what is data. In spite of costing almost 1,000 dollars, many technicians and even end users have the program

THE GIGABYTE OF 1 BILLION BYTES

We, as human beings are accustomed to think in values using the decimal system, having much more facility to deal with numbers using a system based on the number 10. A computer however works with a binary system, and for this reason a Kilobyte does not correspond to 1000 bytes, but to 1024 bytes, so that 1024 is the closest power of 2 to 1000.

A Megabyte corresponds to 1,048,576 bytes and a Gigabyte corresponds to 1,073,741,824 bytes. The problem is that the manufacturers looking to inflate the size of their disks, have a habit of using the decimal system to measure the capacity of disks. Thus, an HD sold as 4.3 Gigabytes instead of having 4,617,089,843 bytes, has only 4.3 billion bytes in the decimal system, that corresponds to little more than 4 Gigabytes in the binary system.

The user, happy with his new 4.3 Gigabyte HD, soon perceives when he installs it that the capacity is only 4 Gigabytes and starts asking where the other 300 Megabytes went. Unhappily this practice has been used by almost all manufacturers, that even have the audacity to write in some HD manuals, if not on the HD itself, a disclaimer such as "The manufacturer reserves the right to consider 1 Gigabyte as 1,000,000,000 bytes".

5 THE MOTHERBOARD

The function of the motherboard is to supply a means by which the processor can communicate as fast as possible and with as much integrity as possible with all the computer's other peripherals. The name motherboard is justified by the fact that all the other components are mounted or connected to it.

Support for new technologies, upgrade possibilities and up to a certain point, even the performance of the equipment are determined by the motherboard.

FORMATS

Motherboards both in the older AT format and also in the newer ATX format are to be found for sale. The two standards differ basically by their physical size: ATX motherboards are much larger which permits designers to create boards with a more rational disposition of the components, avoiding their being too cramped together. The cabinets for ATX motherboards are also bigger permitting better refrigeration.

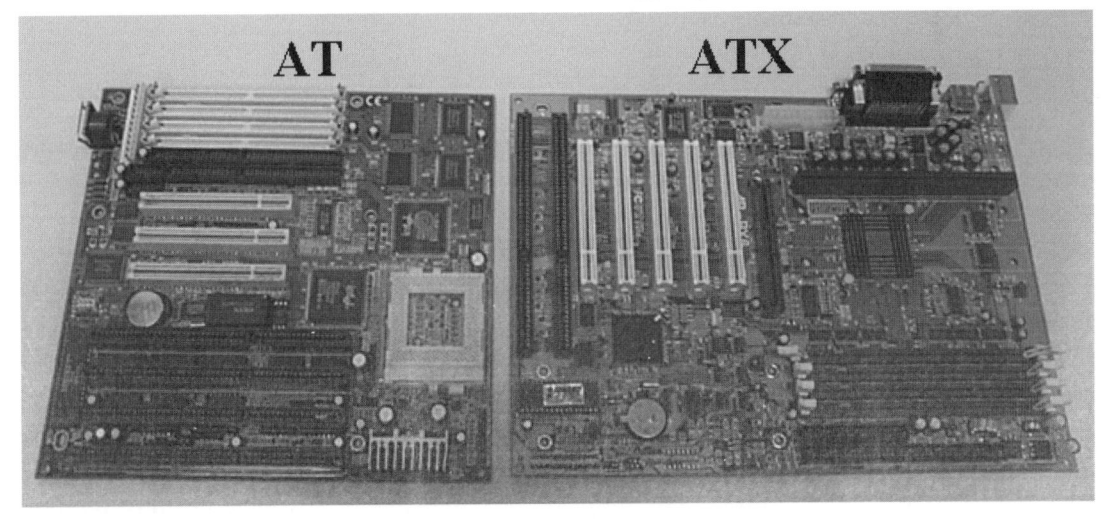

Although you can still find motherboards for both standards the tendency is for the AT format to be replaced by the ATX.

MOTHERBOARD COMPONENTS

Independent of its format or model, we almost always find the same components on a motherboard. We have: ISA, PCI and AGP slots to house sound, video, fax modem cards and others, sockets for memory modules and the processor, serial and parallel ports, diskette drive controller, IDE (hard disk) interfaces, connectors for the keyboard and power supply as well as, of course, the BIOS and the supporting Chipset.

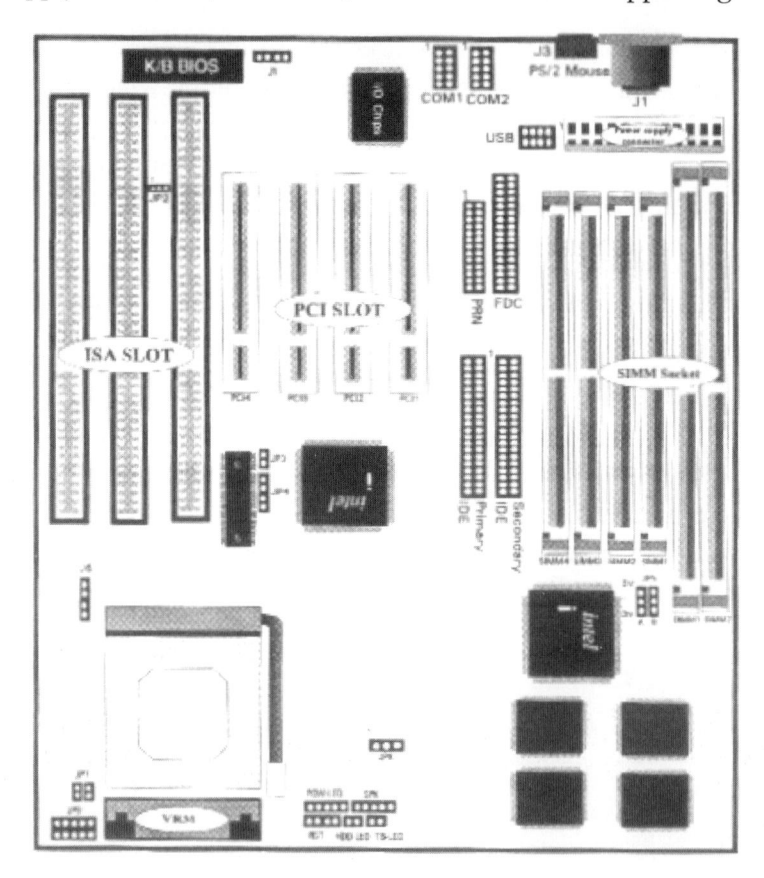

DIAGRAM THAT SHOWS A TYPICAL LAYOUT OF THE COMPONENTS ON A MOTHERBOARD.

CHIPSET

It is safe to say that the chipset is the most important motherboard component, because it is this that controls the flow of data between the processor, the memory and the other components. The ISA, PCI and AGP buses, as well as the IDE interfaces, parallel and serial ports, as well as RAM memory and cache memory are all controlled

The Motherboard

by the chipset.

The chipset is comprised of several other small chips internally, each one with its own function. There is a chip to control the IDE, another for memory etc. This is where it gets its name from. There are various chipset models. The chipsets i430FX, i430HX, i430VX and i430TX made by Intel, as well as others by other manufacturers are used in socket 7 motherboards for example. In the Super 7 motherboards there is a preponderance of Apollo MVP 3, Aladdin V and Sis chipsets, while in Pentium II motherboards the most commonly found chipsets are i440FX, i440LX, i440EX, i440ZX and i440BX.

The Chipset also determines the bus frequencies the motherboard will support and consequently which processors may be used. Pentium II motherboards equipped with the LX chipset for example, are only capable of supporting the Pentium II up to 333Mhz and the Celeron. Motherboards equipped with the BX chipset support a bus frequency of 100 MHz and therefore support all Pentium II processors, as well as the Celeron and the Pentium III.

When you go to buy a motherboard try to find out what chipset it uses and which processors it supports.

BIOS

BIOS is an acronym for "Basic Input Output System". The BIOS is the lowest software level of the system, the closest to the hardware, and is responsible for recognizing the hardware components installed, give the initial boot and provide basic information to enable the computer to function.

The BIOS is recorded in a small chip installed on the mother board. Each BIOS is personalized for a specific model of motherboard, and won't function in any other type.

Like a credit card, or toothbrush, it is personal and non transferable.

Many of the BIOS resources may be configured by the user. To facilitate this task there is one more small program called **Setup**. To enter in Setup press the DEL key while the computer has just been switched on and counting the memory.

When we initialize the system, the BIOS does a memory count, identifies the plug and play devices installed in the motherboard, as well as a general check of other installed components. This procedure is called POST (Power-on Self Test) and is aimed at seeing if there is anything wrong with any component, and to verify if there is anything new installed. Only after the POST has completed successfully does the BIOS hand over control to the Operating system. Then the message "Starting

Windows 98", or any other similar, depending on the operating system that is installed.

L2 CACHE

L2 cache is actually a very important component, without it the performance of the system would fall by up to 40% because of the slow access to the main memory.

Practically all motherboards for 486 and Pentium processors have at least 256Kb or 512KB of cache, while some have 1 MB or even 2 MB.

Some of the slightly older motherboards don't come with any cache, instead there is a slot where a COAST (Cache On a Stick) module may be plugged in. In this case, the cache memory module should be acquired separately. COAST modules are difficult to find and are relatively expensive. A 512 KB module for example costs between $10 and $15.

Although these motherboards with sockets for COAST modules are no longer manufactured, it is very possible that you will encounter them if you work with slightly older computers.

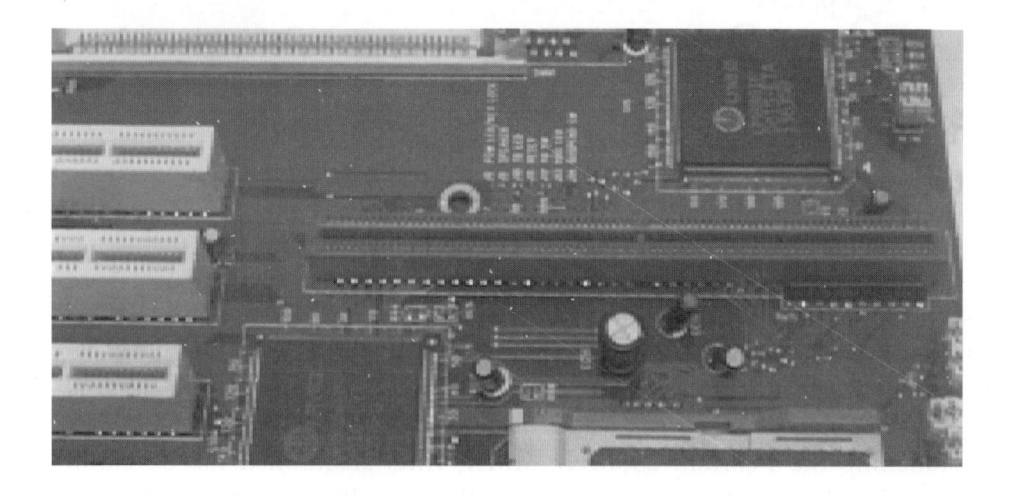

Socket for a COAST module in a 486 motherboard

There are also cases of motherboards with falsified cache chips. These are plastic chips with the appearance of cache memory but with nothing inside, soldered in the motherboard in place of real cache memory modules and the inscription "Write Back" in low relief. In the POST screen which appears soon after the memory counting, but before Windows starts loading the supposed cache is also identified as "Write Back" even if there is not any cache at all. To stop the screen for enough time to read it, press the Pause key when the POST screen begins to appear.

This type of coup was used a lot in the cheaper motherboards, of most those manufactured between 94 and 97. In order to identify a motherboard of this type all you have to do is check if the inscription "Write Back" is stamped on the cache modules, or if the cache is identified as "Write Back" on the POST screen.

PROCESSOR SOCKET

A new type of socket for processors called the ZIF ("Zero Insertion Force" socket) was created as from the 486 processors. The processor may be easily inserted or removed just by lifting the little lever at the side of the socket.

There are variation of ZIF sockets that go from socket 1 up to socket 7. A good way to identify which processors are supported by the motherboard is simply to check which socket is used. This information is to be found stamped in low relief on the socket.

After launching the Pentium 233MHz MMX, Intel abandoned the development of processors for the socket 7, launching the Pentium II which uses a Slot One. To support the new versions of the K6-2 that operate with frequencies of up to 450 MHz and the Cyrix 6x86 MII launched with a clock of up to 300 MHz, a new socket called Super 7 was launched, which, in spite of using the same pin configuration as the old socket 7 and maintaining compatibility with all the processors supported by it, brings support for the resources that the Slot One has, such as a bus 100 MHz, AGP and clock multipliers up to 6x.

The specifications for each socket are:

Type of socket	Number of contacts	Voltages Supported	When it was used	Supported processors
Socket 1	169	5v	First 486 motherboards	486SX, 486DX, 486DX-2
Socket 2	238	5v	First 486 motherboards	486SX, 486DX, 486DX2 e Pentium Overdrive
Socket 3	237	5 and 3.3 V	The majority of 486 motherboards	486DX, 486SX, 486DX2, 486DX4, AMD 5x86, Cyrix 5x86 and Pentium Overdrive
Socket 4	273	5v	First generation of Pentium processors	Pentium from 60 to 66 MHz
Socket 5	320	3.3 V	Some of the older Pentium processors	Pentiums of 75, 90, 100 and 133 MHz, Pentium MMX Overdrive (doesn't support the Pentium 60 and 66 MHz)
Socket 6	235	5 and 3.3 V	Brought some improvements over the Socket 3, but was never used due to its delayed launch	486SX, DX, DX-2, DX-4, Pentium Overdrive
Socket 7	312	Varies between 3.5 e 2.8v	Was the standard until the end of 97	Pentiums from 75 to 200 MHz, 6x86, K5 and K6 (in the case of motherboards with support for 3,3 or 3,5v) and also the Pentium MMX, 6x86MX and the first versions of the 6x86MII and K6-2 (for motherboards that support 2,9 or 2,8v).
Socket Super 7	312	Varies between 3.5 and 2v	Current standard for AMD and Cyrix processors	All the processors supported by socket 7 and the faster versions of the K6-2 and 6x86MII as well as the K6-3
Socket 8	387	3.3 V	Motherboards developed exclusively for the Pentium Pro	Pentium Pro
Slot 1	242	3.3, 2.8 and 2v	Pentium II motherboards	Pentium II, Celeron, Pentium III and Xeon

JUMPERS

Jumpers are small plastic pieces with metal inside which are used to join or not the pins on the motherboard or other cards, functioning as a kind of removable switch.

By varying the position of the jumpers or installing or removing them, it is possible to program different motherboard resources such as the voltage, type and speed of the processor, memory used and others. When a computer is assembled for the first time the motherboard jumpers should be correctly configured for it to function properly, if not, as well as not working, it may even damage some components. Many modern motherboards are "jumperless" that is they don't have any jumpers, all the configuration of the motherboard is done by software in the Setup.

BUSES

Buses are doors through which the processor may communicate with other computer components such as the video card. In speaking of video cards have you ever noticed that all modern video cards are for PCI or AGP slots? And that almost all modems and sound cards use ISA slots? This happens because modems and sound cards are relatively slow devices for which the ISA bus is sufficient. However video cards need a much faster bus which is the reason they use PCI or AGP slots.

I am certain that you are curious to know more details aren't you? Then let's study now the different type of buses that existing.

ISA (INDUSTRY STANDARD ARCHITECTURE) OF 8 BITS

The 8088 processors used in XT micros communicated with their peripherals using binary words of 8 bits. The ISA bus standard of 8 bits was created to be used in conjunction with these processors. This almost pre-historic bus functioned using binary words of 8 bits and a frequency of 8 MHz, a more than sufficient speed for a slow processor like the 8088.

ISA 16 bits

286 processors communicated with other peripherals using 16 bit words. In order to accompany this improvement on the processors part and to permit the use of 16 bit peripherals, there was an extension of the ISA bus standard forming the 16 Bit ISA. This bus, as well as the 286 processor worked with 16 bit words and a frequency of 8 MHz. Although in terms of velocity it is way past obsolete, even the most modern mother boards have ISA slots.

It may seem senseless that a motherboard equipped with the latest technology include a bus as slow and out of date as ISA. The reason is that in spite of being so old, the speed of ISA is more than sufficient to accommodate slow peripherals like modems and sound cards. As there are still large quantities of ISA peripherals in use, all motherboard manufacturers include ISA slots in order to provide compatibility with them. The tendency is that ISA will be extinct within a few years.

ISA Slots. The small one is 8 bits, while the others are 16 Bits.

MCA (MICRO CHANNEL ARCHITECTURE)

With the arrival of 386 processors which worked with 32 bit binary words, it became necessary to create a more advanced Bus than ISA to permit the use of fast peripherals and video cards and hard disk controllers. IBM then created the MCA that functioned with 32 bit words and a speed of 10 MHz permitting the passage of data up to 40 MB/s (megabytes per second)

MCA had a small problem the fact that it was patented by IBM in such a way that only they could use it in their computers. Without no choice, other manufacturers were obliged to produce computers equipped only with ISA slots. This was a big holdback, because, in spite of the 386 being extremely advanced for the time, it ended up being underutilized because of the slow ISA bus, seeing as the other components like hard disks and video cards continued being accessed at the ISA bus speed. The use of such computers was impractical for those who worked with images.

These computers are called "AT 386" or "AT 486", because in spite of using 386 or 486 processors, they use the same bus as used in the AT 286 computers. MCA fell into disuse with the arrival of EISA and VLB.

In spite of bringing surprising resources for the period in which it was launched, like Bus Mastering and Plug-and-Play support (it was the first bus to support these resources, back in 87), MCA was not successful due to it's high cost, incompatibility with ISA and mainly because of its closed architecture.

EISA (EXTENDED ISA)

This new bus was the reply of the other manufacturers, led by Compaq, to MCA, created and patented by IBM.

With the objective of being compatible with ISA, EISA also functioned at 8 MHz, although it worked with 32 bit binary words, giving a transfer speed of 32 MB/s. EISA also offered support for Bus Mastering and Plug-and-Play with an efficiency comparable to MCA.

One of the biggest concerns of the manufacturers during the development of EISA was to maintain compatibility with ISA. The result was a slot with two lines of contacts, capable of supporting EISA cards as well as 8 or 16 bit ISA cards.

An EISA card used all the slot contacts whilst an ISA card only used the first layer. Obviously, EISA was a bus system with enough intelligence to recognize if the card installed was ISA or EISA.

The complexity of EISA ended up in high production costs that made its ready acceptance difficult. In fact, there were few motherboards manufactured with EISA slots and also few expansion cards were developed for this bus. Like MCA EISA is actually considered a dead bus system.

VLB (VESA LOCAL BUS)

Launched in 93 by the Video Electronics Standards Association (an association of the main video card manufacturers), VLB is much faster than EISA or MCA, being used for video cards and hard disk controllers, which had been the principal losers with slow buses. Using VLB hard disks could communicate with the processor at full speed, and this also made the creation of much faster video cards possible.

As before, the main preoccupation was to maintain compatibility with ISA. This was achieved by making the VLB with 3 connectors. The first two are the same as a normal ISA slot, and an ISA card could be installed, the third connector was used by the VLB for the transference of data at the high speeds permitted by the VLB.

VLB functions at the motherboard frequency, for example, in a 486 DX-2 50, where the motherboard functions at 25 MHz, the VLB will function also at 25MHz. And in a 486 DX-4 100 motherboard that functions at 33 MHz the VLB will also function at 33 MHz. It is worthwhile remembering that VLB is a 32 bit bus.

The disadvantages of VLB are the lack of support for Bus Mastering and Plug-and-Play, as well as a high amount of processor utilization and electrical limitations that permit a maximum of 2 or 3 VLB slots per computer. This is not a big limitation because generally only a video card and a super IDE controller card were used in these slots.

Due to its high performance and low cost, and principally due to the support of most of the manufacturers, VLB rapidly became a standard bus for 486 motherboards. As VLB was developed to work in conjunction with 486 processors, it was not further developed for use in Pentium motherboards because its adaptation would generate large costs as well as incompatibility problems.

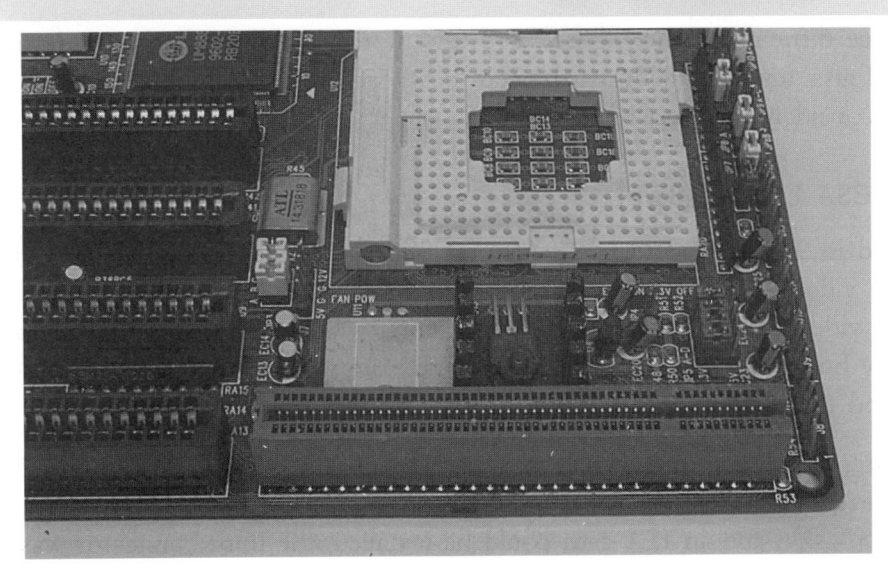

VLB Slots are only found in 486 motherboards.

PCI (PERIPHERAL COMPONENT INTERCONNECTOR)

Created by Intel, PCI is as fast as the VLB, however it is much cheaper and more versatile. Another advantage is that unlike VLB, it is not controlled by the processor, but by a dedicated controller located in the chipset. As well as reducing the demand on the processor it permits that PCI be used in conjunction with any processor without great modifications.

In a Pentium motherboard, PCI functions at half of the motherboard clock speed, that is, it functions at 25 MHz, 30 MHz, or 33 MHz depending on the bus speed used by the motherboard. Functioning at 33MHz for example, PCI permits a data transfer speed of 133 MB/s, 120 MB/s at 30 MHz and 100 MB/s when functioning at 25 MHz. In a Pentium 75, where the motherboard functions at 50 MHz, PCI will function at 25 MHz; in a Pentium 60, 120, 150 or 180, it will run at 30 MHz, and in a Pentium 66, 100, 133, 166, 200 or 233, it will function at 33 MHz. In 486 motherboards PCI functions at the same speed as the bus frequency, that is: 25, 33 or 40 MHz.

As well as cost and speed, PCI possesses other advantages like its native support for plug and play. If new peripherals are installed in PCI slots they will be recognized automatically and configured through the combined efforts of BIOS and an operating system with PnP support such as 95/98.

Actually video cards and disk controllers find it almost obligatory to use the PCI bus. The majority of slower components like sound cards and modems still use the ISA bus, even though these components are finding their way more and more into PCI versions.

PCI slots (white) above an AGP Slot.

AGP (ACCELERATED GRAPHICS PORT)

AGP is a new bus system, tailor made for the newer generation of video cards. It operates at twice the speed of PCI, that is 66 MHz, permitting a data transfer rate of 266 MB/s, two times as fast as PCI.

As well as speed, AGP permits a video card to access RAM memory directly. This is a resource much used in 3D cards where RAM memory is used to store the textures that are applied over the polygons that form the three dimensional image. Even though you are using the PCI bus, it is still possible to use normal memory for storing textures etc within the program, in which case the data have to pass through the processor, downgrading the overall performance of the computer. AGP was originally conceived to equip Pentium II motherboards, but many manufacturers also began to use it in socket 7 motherboards.

It is important not to confuse bus with slots. For example in a motherboard we usually have 4 or 5 PCI slots. All these slots share the same bus of 133 MB/s. The bus is a data highway which permits communication with the processor and is shared by all the other peripherals connected to this bus. Slots are only the means of connection, i.e. sockets.

The 16 MB/s of the ISA bus for example, are shared by all the other peripherals connected in ISA slots, as well as the serial and parallel ports and by the disk controller. The PCI bus is shared by all the other PCI peripherals, by the IDE ports (where the hard disks are connected) and also by SCSI controllers if there happen to be any installed in PCI slots.

The Motherboard

The AGP bus however is only used by the video card which makes a big difference in the case of fast cards such, as 3D cards. In case there are several HDs in the same computer that is equipped with a fast video card in the PCI or ISA slots, the 133Mhz of the PCI bus will be insufficient, and seriously affect the performance of the peripherals connected to it. In this case, the use of an AGP video card is strongly recommended

Actually, modern motherboards come equipped with ISA, PCI and AGP slots. The ISA slot is used for slow peripherals such as modems and sound cards, the PCI for older video cards and SCSI controllers, and the AGP for 3D video cards.

Although an AGP slot may also be used by 2D video cards, this does not bring any advantages because these cards do not use any RAM memory to store textures and are not fast enough to take advantage of the faster AGP speed. It is to be noted therefore, that a 2D video card rigorously follows the same speed as its PCI version.

AGP is a bus destined for use exclusively by video cards. For this reason motherboards come with only one AGP slot.

USB (UNIVERSAL SERIAL BUS)

Until a short time ago we could only count upon the serial and parallel ports for the connection of external devices like mice and printers. But with only two serial ports and one parallel, the possibilities of expansion were quite limited. As well as this, the speed of these interfaces left a lot to be desired.

The USB is an attempt to create a new standard for the connection of external peripherals. Its principal device are the easy of use and the fact that it is possible to connect several peripherals to the same USB port at once.

With the exception of PCMCIA (used in notebooks), USB is the first bus system for computers that really is Plug-and-Play. We can connect peripherals even with the computer switched on, it is only necessary to supply an appropriate device driver for it to function and it is not even necessary to reinitialize the computer. The USB controller also has sufficient intelligence to perceive the disconnection of a peripheral as well.

Although the "boom" has not yet happened, there are already several USB peripherals on the market that range from mice to keyboards and network cards, passing through scanners, printers, Zip drives, video conference cameras and much more.

Although all chipsets as from the i430VX (launched in 96) offer support for the USB, and practically all the motherboards equipped with it offer two USB ports, manufacturers don't usually supply USB sockets due to the little interest in USB at the moment, and these have to be separately acquired. The obvious exception are ATX motherboards which have them built in.

Search on your motherboard for a socket with 10 pins (two rows of five), with the letters USB close to it. If you have the manual, examine the motherboard diagram. Each row of pins is a USB outlet, you just need to connect the appropriate cable.

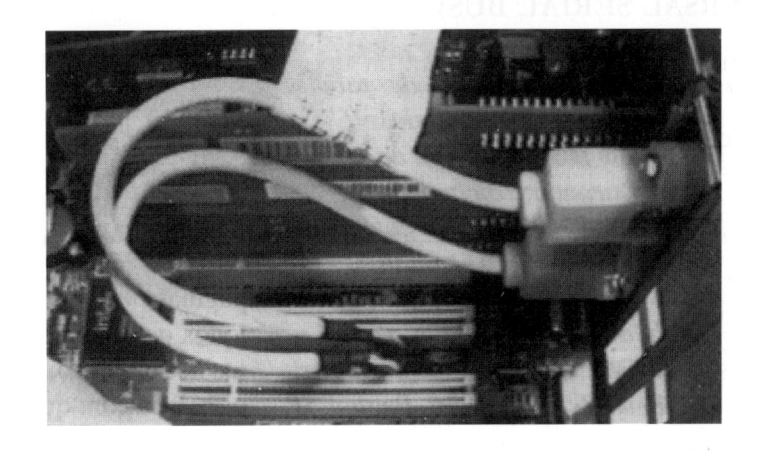

You can connect up to 127 peripherals in series to a single USB port by connecting the first to the USB exit on the motherboard and then connecting the next to this device and so on.

The USB controller is in the root of the bus. In theory we can connect other nodes known as hubs to this. A hub is nothing more than a junction box with more sockets with a limit of 7 per hub. The hub has permission to supply more levels of connections that permits connecting more hubs to the first etc. until the limit of 127 peripherals permitted by the USB is reached. The idea is that larger peripherals such as monitors and printers may serve as hubs, making available several sockets in each one. "USB monitors" are nothing more than normal monitors with an integrated hub.

IRQ (INTERRUPT REQUESTS)

PC type computers have a resource called interrupt request. The function of the interrupt requests is to permit the various devices to solicit services from the processor. There are 16 Interrupt channels called IRQ ("Interrupt Request") that are like strings which a device may pull when it has something to say to the processor. When asked, the processor stops all it is doing to give attention to the device calling it and continuing its work after attending to the request. Two devices cannot share the same interrupt, if this happens we have a hardware conflict. This happens because the processor has no way of knowing which device is calling it, causing all sorts of malfunctioning at random of the devices involved.

64 HARDWARE PC

IRQ addresses are normally configured as follows:

IRQ 0	Used by the motherboard
IRQ 1	Keyboard.
IRQ 2	Used by the motherboard
IRQ 3	Serial Port 1 (Com2 and Com 4)
IRQ 4	Serial Port 2 (Com1 and Com 3)
IRQ 5	Sound card
IRQ 6	Diskette drive
IRQ 7	LPT 1 (Printer port)
IRQ 8	Real time clock
IRQ 9	Vídeo card (not necessary in some motherboards)
IRQ 10	SCSI controller (If you don't have a SCSI card, this stays vacant)
IRQ 11	Available
IRQ 12	USB Connector
IRQ 13	Math co-processor
IRQ 14	Primary IDE controller
IRQ 15	Secondary IDE controller

It is worthwhile remembering that if a certain device have not been installed, then the interrupt destined to this will be vacant. The addresses of installed devices also may be changed, for example if you install a sound card using a different available interrupt, then interrupt 5 may be used by another device.

DMA (DIRECT MEMORY ACCESS)

DMA seek to improve the general performance of the computer, by permitting peripherals to transfer data directly to memory, saving the processor from one more task.

There are 8 DMA ports and as happens with interrupt requests, two devices may not share the same DMA Channel, otherwise there would be a conflict. The 8 DMA channels are numbered from de 0 to 7, channels 0 to 3 make data transfer using 8 bits and the other four use 16 bits. The use of 8 bit binary words by the first four DMA channels is in order to maintain compatibility with older peripherals.

Because they are much slower, DMA Channels are used only for slow peripherals like diskette drives, sound cards, and ECP parallel ports. Faster peripherals use Bus Mastering, which is a type of improved DMA.

DMA channel 2 is natively used by the diskette controller. A sound card usually needs two DMA channels, one of 8 bits and the other of 16 bits, normally using DMA 1 and 5. DMA 4 is reserved for the motherboard. This leaves us with channels 3, 6 and 7 free. In case the parallel port is configured in the Setup to operate in ECP mode, we will need a DMA for it also, but it can be configured to use channel 3.

DMA 0	Available
DMA 1	Sound Card
DMA 2	Diskette drive controller
DMA 3	ECP Parallel port
DMA 4	Used by the mother board
DMA 5	Sound card
DMA 6	Available
DMA 7	Available

PLUG-AND-PLAY

The objective of this standard is to make the computer capable of detecting and automatically configuring any peripheral that is installed, reducing the work required of the user to just physically installing the new component.

In spite of being an old idea (MCA launched in 87 already possessed PnP support) it is only in recent years that PnP has turned popular. The difficulty is that as well as a compatible bus, it is necessary to have support from the BIOS, the operating system and also on behalf of the peripherals for everything to function.

Everything begins during the initialization of the computer. The BIOS sends an interrupt signal to all the peripherals installed in the computer. A PnP peripheral is capable of responding to this signal, thus permitting the BIOS to recognize the PnP devices that are installed.

The following step is to create a table with all the available interrupts and assign each one to a device. The operating system enters into the scene soon afterwards and being capable of working cooperatively with the BIOS, receives the information about the system configuration and supplying all the low level software (in the form of device drivers) necessary for the device to be utilized by programs.

Information about the actual configuration and distribution of the resources between the components is recorded in an area of CMOS called ESCD. Both the BIOS during the POST, as well as the operating system during initialization, read this list and, in case there have been no changes in installed hardware, maintain their configurations. This permits the operating system (as long as it is compatible with PnP) to alter the configurations whenever necessary. In Windows 98, the user himself may freely alter the system configurations using the Control Panel.

Actually, only Windows 95 and 98 are compatible with Plug-and-Play. Some systems like Windows NT 4 offer a limited compatibility, whilst others, like Windows 3.11 and Linux don't offer any support at all.

Problems with Plug-and-Play

The way in which Plug-and-Play was implemented in microcomputers should permit (at least in theory), good functioning. The problem is that not all peripherals used at the moment are compatible with PnP (older sound cards and modems for example), whiles some are only partially compatible (many current sound cards and modems, serial and parallel ports amongst others). These peripherals are called "Legacy ISA".

AS the BIOS doesn't have the means to identify which resources are being occupied by these peripherals, it is quite likely that it may attribute the same values for other PnP devices, causing conflicts.

To avoid this problem it is necessary to manually reserve the IRQ and DMA addresses used by legacy devices through a "PNP/PCI Setup", which is part of the CMOS Setup. If for example you have a non PnP sound card, that is configured (by jumpers) to use IRQ 5 and DMA channels 1 and 5, you should reserve these three channels so that the bios does not attribute them to any other device. Setting the option to "Yes" leaves the channel reserved and setting it to "No/ICU" leaves it free for use by PnP peripherals.

The Motherboard

```
        ROM PCI/ISA BIOS (<PZL97>)
             PNP AND PCI SETUP
            AWARD SOFTWARE, INC.

PNP OS Installed    : Yes          DMA 1 Used By ISA : No/ICU
Slot 1 (RIGHT) IRQ  : Auto         DMA 3 Used By ISA : No/ICU
Slot 2 IRQ          : Auto         DMA 5 Used By ISA : No/ICU
Slot 3 IRQ          : Auto
Slot 4/5 (LEFT) IRQ : Auto         ISA MEM Block BASE : No/ICU
PCI Latency Timer   : 32 PCI Clock
                                   SYMBIOS SCSI BIOS  : Auto
                                   USB IRQ            : Disabled
IRQ  3 Used By ISA : No/ICU
IRQ  4 Used By ISA : No/ICU
IRQ  5 Used By ISA : No/ICU
IRQ  7 Used By ISA : No/ICU
IRQ  9 Used By ISA : No/ICU
IRQ 10 Used By ISA : No/ICU
IRQ 11 Used By ISA : No/ICU
IRQ 12 Used By ISA : No/ICU         ESC : Quit          ↑↓←→ : Select Item
IRQ 14 Used By ISA : No/ICU         F1  : Help          PU/PD/+/- : Modify
IRQ 15 Used By ISA : No/ICU         F5  : Old Values   (Shift)F2 : Color
                                    F6  : Load BIOS Defaults
                                    F7  : Load Setup Defaults
```

The "PnP/PCI Setup" screen of an Award BIOS Setup

Windows 95/98 possesses some routines that permit these peripherals to be identified in an indirect manner, configuring them and saving the configurations in the ESCD. This verification is made during the "Add New Hardware" routines.

Although it is not infallible, this resource significantly reduces the conflicts generated by older peripherals.

6 VIDEO CARDS AND MONITORS

The function of the video card is to construct the images that will be shown on the monitor which is the main means of communication between the user and the computer.

Not many years ago it was common to find computers equipped only with a CGA (Color Graphics Array) video card and monitors which as well as being of very low quality didn't permit the use of a graphics interface. To our great relief, the video cards as well as other computer components also evolved in an incredible way in these last two decades, permitting us to have practically perfect images instead of those horrible green monitor images.

There have been video cards created using almost every type of bus that exists from ISA to PCI, passing through MCA, EISA and VLB. Nowadays, however, we use only PCI or AGP video cards with a growing predominance for AGP cards that are faster because they use a more modern type of bus.

It is even possible to use an ISA video card in conjunction with Windows 98, however these cards are extremely slow, which negatively affects the overall performance of the system.

VIDEO MEMORY

The video card uses a special type of memory called video memory to store the image to be shown on the screen. This memory stores the image to be shown on the screen and is constantly updated by the video card seeing that the image to be shown changes constantly every time the mouse is moved or a new window is opened for example.

Many people think that the more memory a video card has the faster it will be, but that is not true. The quantity of memory only determines the resolution and the number of colors that may be exhibited by Windows or other applications. A card with 1 megabyte of memory, for example, will be capable of exhibiting 16 million colors with a resolution of 640x480 or 65 thousand colors with a resolution of 800x600. A card with 2 megabytes would be capable of showing 16 million colors with a resolution of 800x600.

To save you from making the calculations here is a table showing how much memory is needed for each resolution:

HARDWARE PC

Resolution	No of points	No of color bits per point	No of colors	Memory used
640x480	307.200	4	16	150 KB
640x480	307.200	8	256	300 KB
640x480	307.200	16	65 K	600 KB
640x480	307.200	24	16 million	900 KB
800x600	480.000	4	16	234 KB
800x600	480.000	8	256	468 KB
800x600	480.000	16	65 K	937 KB
800x600	480.000	24	16 million	1.406 KB
1024x756	786.432	4	16	384 KB
1024x756	786.432	8	256	768 KB
1024x756	786.432	16	65 K	1.536 KB
1024x756	786.432	24	16 million	2.304 KB
1280x1024	1.310.720	4	16	640 KB
1280x1024	1.310.720	8	256	1.280 KB
1280x1024	1.310.720	16	65 K	2.560 KB
1280x1024	1.310.720	24	16 million	3.840 KB

It is worth remembering that the higher the resolution and quantity of colors, the lower will be the performance of the card because the quantity of data to be processed will be more. You may alter the resolution and number of colors to be used by Windows by means of the windows "Video Properties". To access it, just right click on a blank part of the screen and choose "properties" from the menu that arises.

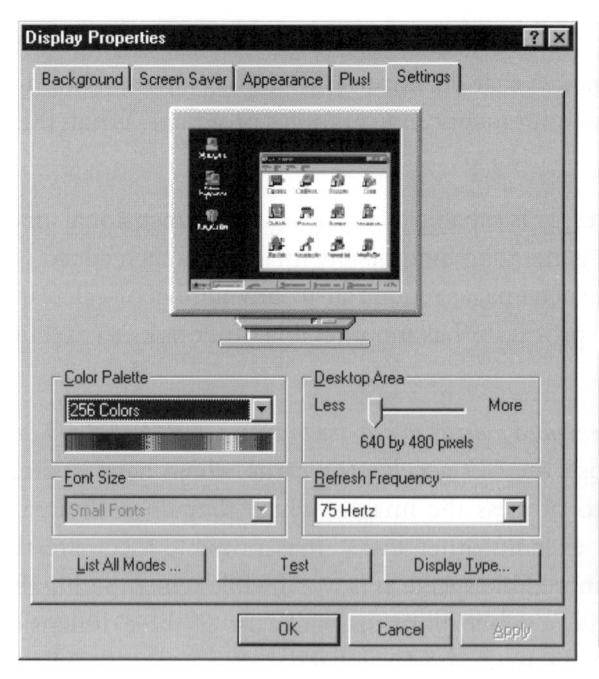

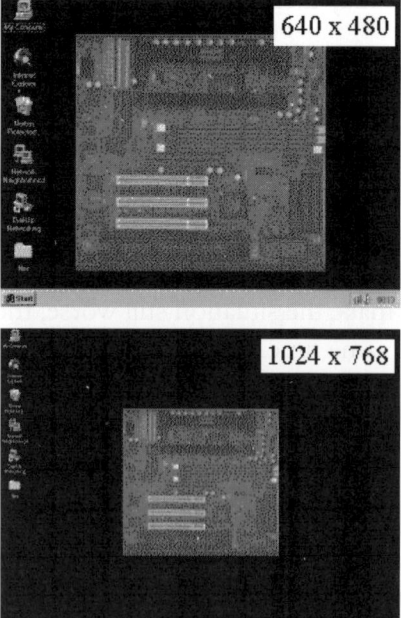

3D VIDEO CARDS

The function of a 3D video card is to help the processor in displaying 3 dimensional images. An image with three dimensions is formed by innumerable polygons upon which are applied textures. To represent the image of a table in 3D for example, whether in a game or graphics program the program needs to keep in its the locations of the various polygons that make up the table together with the textures that will be applied to them memory. Also its necessary to calculate the exact position of each polygon in the image, the illumination points and the non-visible parts of the image.

Although a little complicated and very laborious, this process rewards us with almost perfect three dimensional images.

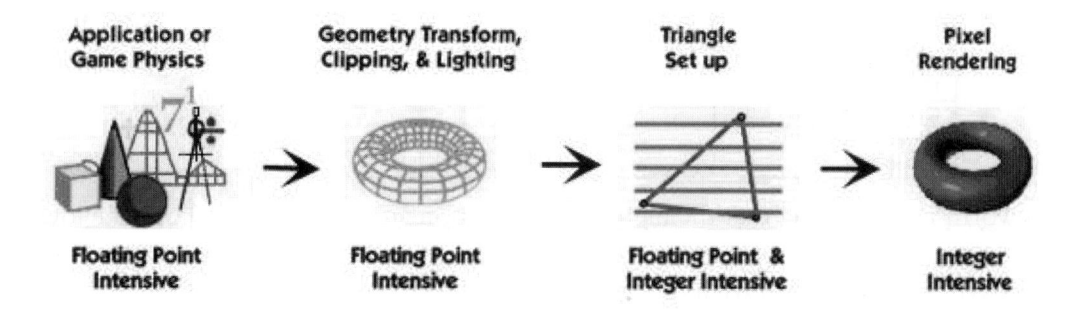

Functions executed by a 3D accelerator card *(courtesy of Advanced Micro Devices Inc.)*

You may then ask:

There are many three dimensional games that do not use 3D cards, such as Doom, FX Fighter, Duke Nukem, Quake, etc., without mentioning graphics programs. What, then, is the necessity of a 3D card?

The answer is that, although the processor is capable of creating three dimensional images, working by itself it is not capable of generating high quality images at a high speed (such as those demanded by games) because such images require an absurd number of calculations To make the situation still worse, the processor has innumerable other tasks to execute at the same time.

Somebody then thought: *"What if we created a device to help the processor create perfect 3D images and at a high speed?"* From there arose the 3D accelerator cards which have dedicated processors whose only function is to process the images, which they do with amazing speed, freeing up the processor to execute other tasks. It is possible to create three dimensional images with them at an incredible speed. It is worthwhile remembering that a 3D video card only improves the image in applications that make use of three dimensional images and in 2D applications the card remains under utilized.

HOW IT FUNCTIONS

An image in 3 dimensions is formed by thousands of small triangles or other polygons. When the program needs to move the image, the corners of the object are moved, thus giving the sensation of movement. However, using polygons, we only have the outlines of the objects.

To make the image more realistic, textures are applied to the polygons. Textures are nothing more than 2 dimensional images that are molded to the designed objects giving a much more realistic sensation. To simulate a wall for example we may apply a photo taken of a real wall onto the polygons that permits an almost perfect image. The texture application is called rendering.

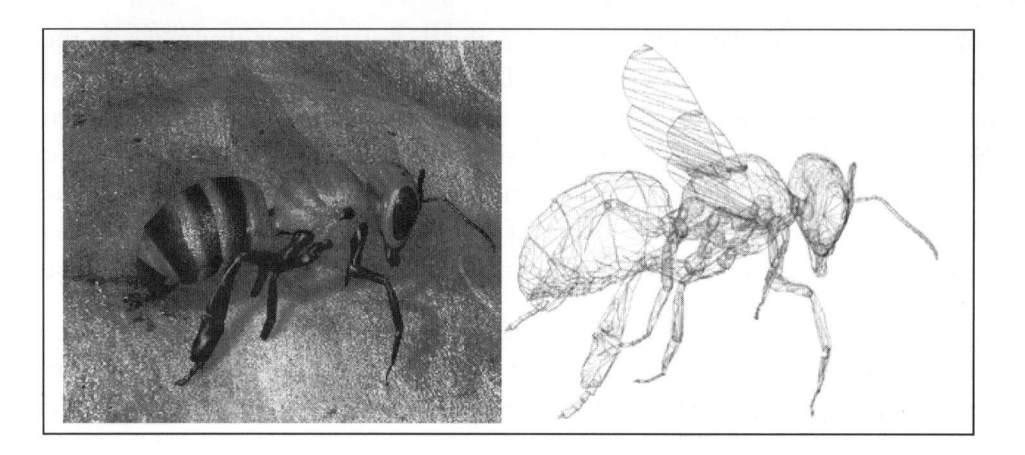

(Image courtesy of NVIDIA Corporation)

It is obvious that when the images are moved, the textures are moved together with the polygons. The bigger the number and size of the textures, the greater the speed of the processor and 3D accelerator will have to be.

Video memory will also store the textures that make up image in the case of 3D video cards. Although the card can use RAM memory to store textures whenever necessary, main memory is very slow if compared to video memory. Exhibition of the images will become slower if more system memory is used to store textures.

For this reason, unlike what happens in 2D cards, the amount of memory in a 3D card directly affects its performance in games that make heavy use of it, because it avoids using system memory.

16Mb is still more than enough to run any modern game with exceptional quality, although you can find 32Mb cards on the market.

MONITORS

The monitor is of a vital importance because together with the video card it forms the principal means of communication between the computer and us. The factors that

Video Cards and Monitors

differentiate the innumerable models for sale on the market are basically the size, the Dot Pitch (the size of the dots that comprise the image), the supported resolutions and the refresh rate of the image.

The size is measured in inches diagonally. The most commonly used at the moment are still 14" and 15" monitors, but in case you want to work with graphics applications or even to use the computer for games, a 17" monitor would be more beneficial. As well as physical size, the advantage of larger monitors is that they invariably support higher resolutions as well as faster refresh rates.

Another important detail in relation to monitors is the size of the dots that make up the image on the screen; this is called the Dot Pitch (DP). If you take a magnifying glass and examine the screen of your monitor you will see that the image is formed by red, green and blue dots, grouped together in threes. The size of this group is known as the dot pitch. The most commonly found dot pitch in most monitors is .29mm squared. Some more recent monitors however use smaller dots, of .22mm or even .19mm. that guarantees a better quality. However avoid some older monitors that used a dot pitch of .39 because the image of these is not good.

A good 14" monitor should support resolutions up to 1024x756 dots. Larger monitors should be capable of showing resolutions of 1280x1024 or even 1600x1200 in the case of a 20" monitor.

A resolution of 800x600 is the most commonly used by users that have 14" monitors, because, even when supported higher resolutions, which result in a smaller image, are uncomfortable in a small monitor. In the case of larger monitors, however, the use of higher resolutions is strongly recommended,.

The last characteristic, and maybe the most important when dealing with monitors, is the frequency with which the image is updated, or the "refresh rate". An electron beam constantly bombards the screen of a monitor forming the image. The number of times per second that this beam updates the image is called the refresh rate. A good monitor should be capable of updating the image at least 75 times per second (75Hz). However sometimes lower quality monitors are only capable of a refresh rate of Hz that causes the so called "flicker" of the image.

Flicker occurs due to the short persistence time of the phosphorus cells on the monitor screen. When using a refresh rate of less than 75Hz the time for the electron beam to rescan is very long (relatively), causing the cells to lose part of their brilliance, suddenly relighting the next time the electron beam passes. This makes the cells flicker, and the image appears unstable. This instability as well as being uncomfortable, is bad for the eyes.

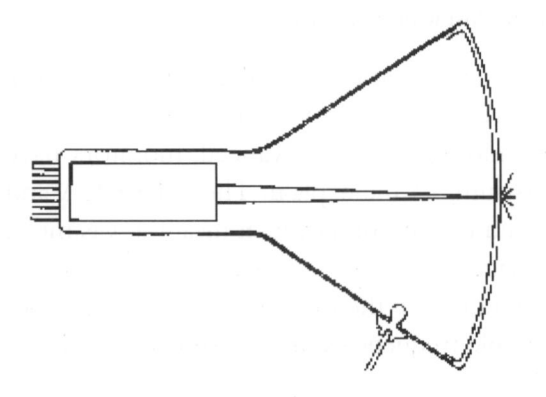

In a monitor an electron beam bombards the luminous cells forming the image. The frequency with which the image is updated is called the refresh rate

The refresh rate of the monitor also depends on the resolution used. The image is updated line by line, from top to bottom in the monitor. The number of lines that the monitor is capable of displaying per second is called the horizontal frequency, and is measured in KHz. 14" monitors normally have a horizontal frequency of 49 KHz, that is to say, they are capable of updating 49 thousand lines per second. This is sufficient when we use a resolution of 640 x 480 or even 800x600 because 49 kHz is enough for a refresh rate of 75 Hz which is an optimum value.

You may ask why it is 75Hz when 49.000 / 600 gives 81,6. The reply is in the horizontal and vertical retrace, which is the time needed for the electron beam to return to the top of the screen from the bottom, or from the end of a line to the beginning of the next. Time lost with retrace varies from monitor to monitor but normally uses up a little more than 5% of the total time. Although smaller monitors generally support a resolution of 1024x768, this is not recommendable as the monitor would not be capable of maintaining a refresh rate of more than 60Hz, thus generating flicker. Larger monitors may have horizontal frequencies of more than 135 kHz, giving us a good refresh rate, even in the highest resolutions.

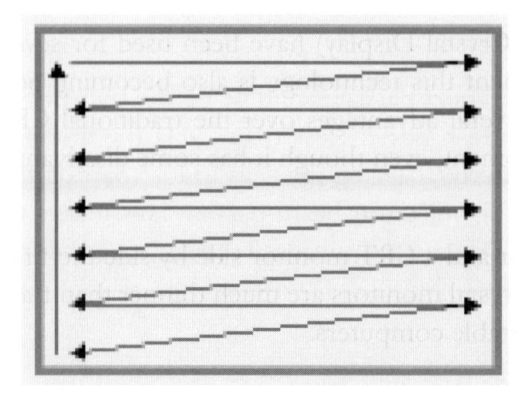

Path traced out by the electron beam each time the image is updated on the screen. The diagonal lines, and the vertical one represent time lost with the retrace.

A curious fact about monitors used at the moment is that they are all actually analogical, whereas the older CGA and EGA monitors were digital. At first this appears crazy, it seems i am trying to say that instead of technology having advanced, monitors have regressed ? Before you put me in a lunatic asylum, let me explain: The older CGA and EGA monitors worked with a much smaller number of colors which meant it was much easier to use digital signals to make up the image. As from the VGA standard analogue signals began to be used permitting the generation of a theoretically unlimited number of colors, because there is no limit to the possible frequencies of an analogue signal.

In practice there can be 256 colors in a VGA monitor and up to 16 million in a super VGA monitor, from any point of view, nothing modest if compared to the older monitors. Obviously, the image to be displayed is stored in the video card memory in a digital format, for example if we configure the video resolution to be 640x480 with 16 color bits we would use 600K bytes of video memory. There is, however, a special circuit called "RAMDAC" (Random Access Memory Digital Analog Converter) in the video card that converts the digital signals into analogue signals that can be understood by the monitor. The function of this circuit is only to read the memory video contents, convert it to an analogue signal and send it to the monitor. Every VGA or SVGA video card includes this circuit.

In saying that current models are analogue, I am referring to the fact that the signals that go from the video card to the monitor are analogue. If you have a look in computer shops, or even in the classified ads of newspapers or computer magazines, you will see many offers of supposedly digital monitors. This is only marketing hype. The only thing digital in these monitors are the controls. Instead of using a knob which you turn to adjust the image, they use touch buttons as in television sets, that is to say "Digital controls". We should not confuse the term "monitor with digital controls" with the term "digital monitor": there is a big difference.

LCD MONITORS

LCD monitors (Liquid Crystal Display) have been used for several decades in portable computers. At the moment this technology is also becoming popular even for desktop computers. LCD has several advantages over the traditional CRT (Cathode Ray Tube) monitors used at the moment, even though it has some disadvantages, especially the high price.

Putting an LCD monitor and a CRT monitor side by side the first difference that strikes you is the size. Liquid Crystal monitors are much thinner than traditional monitors which explains their use in portable computers.

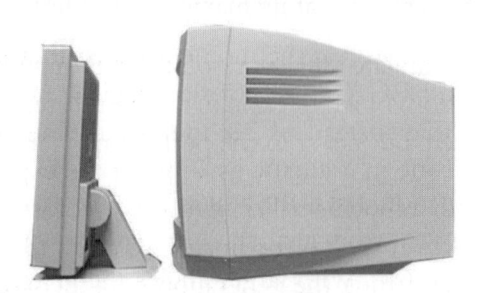

Another advantage of LCD monitors is that they have a truly flat screen that eliminates the distortion caused by the curved screen of a CRT monitor, and increases the useful surface area of the monitor, seeing as to how there is no space lost in the corners of the image. In the illustration below for example, we have a 12' LCD monitor beside a traditional 14" monitor. Note that although the LCD monitor is much smaller, the visible area is almost the same as a 14" monitor.

A 14" LCD monitor has a visible area greater than a 15" CRT monitor, whilst a 15" LCD display has an area almost equal to that of a traditional 17" monitor.

Liquid crystal monitors also use less electricity. Whilst a traditional 14" monitor consumes approximately 90 W, an LCD hardly reaches 40W. Another advantage is that these monitors emit a much smaller quantity of damaging radiation,which makes them especially attractive to those whospend a lot of time daily in front of the monitor.

A disadvantage of LCD monitors is that they are only capable of working at one resolution. In traditional monitors, although there is a maximum limit to resolution, we can freely alternate among lower resolutions. We can freely use 800x600 or 640x480 in a monitor with a maximum resolution of 1024x768 for example, but this is not possible in an LCD monitor that functions correctly only at its maximum resolution

Generally it is possible to simulate smaller resolutions though increasing the image size (which causes a little distortion) or a reduction in the useful area, making the image occupy only the center of the screen, but never in the perfect manner as in CRT monitors.

Another problem with these monitors is the limited angle of vision. Whilst using traditional monitors, the image can be seen from almost any angle, but with LCD monitors the angle of vision is limited to 45° or 60°. With larger angles the image tends to disappear or to have its colors altered. This problem tends to be corrected with the evolution of this technology.

Although they leave nothing to be desired in terms of image quality and have some interesting advantages, LCD monitors are still extremely expensive. The cheapest models available cost approximately 800 dollars, and are therefore are restricted to areas where their advantages overcome the high price.

HOW AN LCD FUNCTIONS

In conventional monitors there is a cathode ray tube in which an electron beam constantly bombards the luminous cells on the screen, thus forming the image. A different technology is used in an LCD monitor that consists in the use of liquid crystals to form the image.

Liquid crystals are substances that mix the characteristics of solids and liquids. Although they are originally transparent, which these substances may have their molecular orientation altered by an electric field, that makes them assume different tones of color according to the intensity of the electric field.

To make a liquid crystal screen, a fine layer of liquid crystals is placed between two thin sheets of glass. In turn, this sandwich is placed between two layers of a polarizing element. A light source is placed behind this screen generally comprised of fluorescent lamps, that emit very little heat, and this provides screen illumination.

In the case of monochrome LCD monitors there is only one layer of crystals that may vary their tones of gray between black and white. In colored monitors three layers of liquid crystal are used, one red, one green and one blue, superimposed on each other. With the illumination from the fluorescent lamp, the colors mix, forming different colors according to the tonality of each layer.

There are at present two technologies used in the fabrication of LCD screens, known as passive matrix (DSTN) and active matrix (TFT). Passive matrix screens possess a more restricted angle of vision, and a longer time for the image to be updated. Whilst in a CRT monitor it takes approximately 30 or 40 milliseconds to change a color, a passive matrix

LCD monitor needs 150 or even 250 milliseconds. For this reason it is difficult to see a mouse cursor on a notebook screen or even to run programs or games that require image rapid changes in an acceptable form. The actual image in these monitors presents an inferior quality due to the low contrast. Active matrix LCDs present a much superior quality with an image refresh time close to that of CRT monitors, a greater angle of vision, and with a much greater contrast. TFT screens are also thinner and lighter

Unlike modern CRTs, all liquid crystal monitors are digital. As all video cards send analogue signals to the monitor, a new circuit is used that converts analogue signals sent by the video card back to the digital format that is understood by the monitor.

The transformation digital-analogue-digital is totaly unnecessary in this case and serves only to degrade the quality of the image and increase the number of circuits used in the monitor, increasing its price. According to the manufacturer, the cost of LCD monitors could be reduced by more than 100 dollars with the use of video cards with digital output.

7 CD-ROMs, Sound Cards, Modems, Printers and Scanners

We have already studied how all the basic components of a PC function: processor, motherboard, hard disks, memory, video cards and monitors. To finalize the theoretical part of this book I am now going to talk a little about CD-ROMs and DVD-ROMs, sound cards, modems, printers and scanners

CD-ROM

The Compact Disc or simply CD, was developed to record music and replace the old vinyl records with its advantages. As the sound on a CD is recorded in a digital format, we have a sound completely free from noise or scratches, with an almost perfect quality.

It did not take long for the manufacturers to see that with a little bit of effort, CDs could also be used to store data. Then the CD-ROM, or "Compact Disc Read Only Memory" was soon created.

The CD-ROM is a disk about 12 cm, or 4.75" in diameter, with little more than 1.2 mm thick and composed of three principal layers. The central layer, also called the reflective layer, is a fine layer of aluminum, silver or even gold where the holes are made wich store the data. In order to protect this very fine and sensitive layer there is on one side a cover of polycarbonate (a type of resistant plastic) 1.2mm thick, on one side and on the other a layer of varnish, wich protects it.

```
                                    → varnish
                                    → reflective layer

                                    → polycarbonate (with a
                                      thickness of 1.2mm)
```

Contrary to what people are accustomed to thinking, the reflective layer is not in the middle of the layer of plastic like a sandwich, but above it, as in a pizza. It is for this reason that the protecting layer of varnish is applied above it. If you make a small scratch on the lower side of the disk the CD-ROM will probably continue to be read normally, as long as the reflective layer where the data is stored was not reached, and although the scratch makes it more difficult to read, the drive will still manage to read the CD by varying the angle of the laser beam. If, however, we scratched the upper surface of the disk, the CD would probably be rendered unusable as the data layer would be damaged.

The recording technique used in making CDs reminds us a little of the old vinyl records consisting in the stamping of the reflective layer (before encapsulation) in a mold. It is for this reason that commercially sold CD-ROMS are also known as stamped CDs and it is impossible to alter their content, seeing as to how there is no way to erase the holes made in the reflective layer.

As well as stamped CDs there are also recordable CDs that are sold as blank CDs and may be recorded once only in a CD-ROM recorder (also known as a burner), instead of stamping the CD in a press, the data is recorded by a stronger laser beam that burns some points in the CD, creating the pits. There are also rewriteable CDs, wich, like a diskette, may be written to and rewritten several times using a CD-RW.

A good quality CDROM may last more than a century as long it is well cared for. As well as taking care not to scratch it, you should avoid exposing it to the sun or other heat sources because the heat may melt the reflective layer, ruining the CD. Recorded CDs are especially sensitive.

The first CD-ROM drives were capable of reading data at 150KBs. The next generation was capable of reading them at twice this speed, 300KB. These new drives then became known as CD-ROMs 2X seeing as they were twice as fast as the originals. Subsenquently, drives began to appear with reading rates of 600 KB/s or 900 KB/s, being called 4X and 6X respectively. A 32X drive should be capable of reading data at 4800 KB/s and so on.

DVD

DVD was originally conceived to store films and replace the video cassette. In spite of its enormous capacity, a normal CD can only store a few minutes of video, whereas a DVD may store more than 2 hours of video with a resolution of 500 lines, more than double that of a video cassette. Another interesting resource is the ability to store up to 8 sound tracks and 32 sub-titles together with the film.

There are four types of DVD that differ in capacity. DVD 5 is capable of storing 4.7 GB of data or 133 minutes de video. DVD 10 uses the same technology as DVD 5 but both sides of the disk are used, thus doubling the capacity, giving 9.4 GB of data or 266 minutes of video. There is also DVD 9 and DVD 18 wich are capable of storing 8.5 and 17 GB data respectively.

A DVD is very similar to a normal CD, the difference is in the pits in the media being much smaller and closer to each other. Whilst in a CD, each optical bit measures 0.83 nm (nanometer) in length and 1.6 nm in width, in a DVD this pit measures only 0.4 nm x 0.74 nm, thus permitting much more data to be recorded in the same physical space.

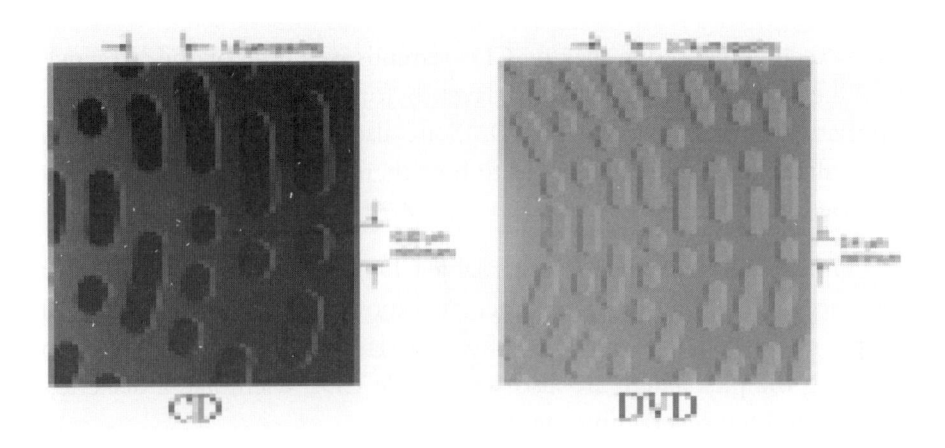

CD   DVD

SOUND CARDS

The PC has an extremely limited sound capacity because the processor can only work with zeros and ones. Every Pc comes with a small built-in loudspeaker that is connected directly to a pair of pins on the motherboard. The sounds emitted by the loudspeaker are generated by the processor wich only knows how to deal with binary numbers, only being able to combine various sequences of 1 and 0 bits to generate rudimentary sounds, like beeps and other noises, wich are generally only used to call the attention of the user when something goes wrong.

On the other hand, an analogue sound has a wave format that may assume an unlimited number of frequencies. Analogue apparatuses, like cassette decks, limit themselves to capturing this signal and transforming it into a magnetic signal with louder or softer passages, depending on the loudness of the sound. When a tape is played back this magnetic signal is converted into an electrical signal that moves the cones of a loudspeaker thus producing sound. This is relatively simple.

However a computer cannot work with analogue signals, and to try to represent real sounds in the form of a sequence of ones and zeros as in the sounds generated by the loudspeaker would be simply ridiculous. Then the idea arose of converting the analogue signal into the digital format through the taking of samples. Imagine that this sound wave was plotted on a Cartesian graph and at each point where the wave passes it received values of X and Y.

We could then take samples of this wave and attribute a numeric value to each one that would represent its position on the graph. The greater the sampling rate, the greater would be the sound quality. The amplitude of the signal is also important, that is the quantity of different values that it may have. For example if we used 8 bits to represent the amplitude of each sample, it would only be possible to represent 256 different tones. If we were to use 16 bits, it would possible to have 65.000 different values and so on.

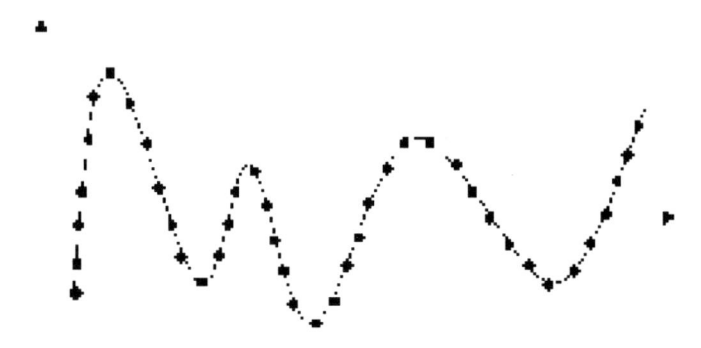

A telephone signal for example is transported between digital exchanges in a format with a sample rate of 8000 samples per second, and an amplitude of 8 bits resulting in a clear sound but with low quality. The sound on a CD is recorded with a sample rate of 44,100 samples per second and an amplitude of 16 bits, that permits 65,000 different values. With a CD we have an almost perfect sound such that an average person is unable to distinguish recorded sound from the live sound.

GENERATING DIGITAL SOUND

What makes the conversion of the analogue signal into digital sound is a circuit called ADC (Analogue Digital Converter). Basically, an ADC extracts samples of an electric wave generated by an analogue device such as a microphone and transforms them into digital signals. These signals may be easily manipulated by the processor and transmitted like any other type of data, permitting you to converse with other people via Internet, for example.

When it is necessary to play a previously recorded sound, we need to do the opposite, that is transform the samples back into an analogue wave that may be played through the loudspeakers connected to the sound card. This conversion is made by the DAC (Digital Analog Converter). The ADC and the DAC are two of the basic components of a sound card.

EXTERNAL CONNECTORS

The sockets found in the back of the sound card are very similar for most makes of sound cards.:

Line Out and Speaker Out: Any sound generated by the sound card is sent to these sockets. The difference between them is that Line Out is not amplified (being at a standard audio level of 100mv) and used for earphones or amplified loudspeakers, whilst the Speaker Out is amplified, and suitable for use with normal (non amplified) loudspeakers.

MIC: This socket is destined to the connection of a microphone, that together with a recording program, like Sound Recorder of Windows may be used for voice recordings. The most interesting application, however, is the possibility of conversing live, like a telephone, via Internet using programs like Net Meeting or Net Phone.

Line In: Various audio apparatuses like a walkman, television set, or video cassette recorder with a Line Out may be connected to this socket, and it is therefore possible to digitalize any sound from these types of equipment.

Joystick: Every sound card also has a built in connector for a joystick. This is the socket on the back part of the sound card with 15 pins.

CD In: This is a small socket, usually White, with 4 pins located on the sound card itself. In order to listen to Audio CDs, the CD-ROM drive should be connected to this using the cable that comes with the CD drive. Without this connection the sound card continues functioning normally, but you won't be able to hear music CDs.

MODEMS

There is nothing more logical than using telephone lines which almost everybody has to communicate between computers. However, there is a small problem with using telephone lines: Computers work with digital signals in which information is stored and processed in the form of 0s and 1s. Telephone lines however are analogue, being adequate for the human voice which can tolerate interference but not suitable for data transmission.

Modems were created for this reason, to permit communication between computers using ordinary telephone lines. Modem is an acronym derived from **Mo**dulator -**dem**odulator and refers to a device wich is capable of transforming digital signals into analogue signals that can be transmitted by telephone lines and afterwards be converted back into digital signals at the other end by the modem receiver.

Modems have shown a notable evolution in the last decade. The first models were only capable of transmitting 300 data bits per second whilst the models available nowadays are capable of maintaining connections at velocities of up to 56 Kbits per second.

Hardmodems vs Softmodems

There are two basic types of modems wich, in spite of having the same function, operate in quite different ways. Modems traditionally had all the necessary components for their functioning leaving the processor only with the task of telling them what to do. These "full" modems are called **hardmodems**. As well as traditional modems there are **softmodems** or **winmodems** to be found on the market, wich operate via software and don't have many of the components found in conventional modems, especially the UART wich co-ordinates the sending and receiving of data. These modems only function with the installation of a program wich is supplied together with the modem.

As they don't have many components, these modems are much cheaper, and it is possible to find one such as a Pctel, 56k, V.90 for less than US$ 20, whilst a 56k US Robotics hardmodem costs at least 80 or 90 dollars. The program functions as a kind of emulator, making the processor execute functions that would normally be executed by the modem itself, like controlling the sending and receiving of signals, error control etc. Of course the computer will be a bit slower than normal while the modem is being used, seeing that as well as its normal functions, the processor has to do the modem's processing. The minimum processor recommended by the manufacturers in order to use a softmodem is a Pentium 100. Softmodems also tend to be more susceptible to line noise or poor quality lines where they present a performance inferior to hardmodems.

To check whether your modem is a softmodem, just have a look at the Box it came in, or the instruction manual, and see it if says that you need a Pentium processor of any model, or that the modem only functions with Windows, if so, then you are dealing with a softmodem. One more clue is that almost all modems that use PCI slots are softmodems.

Another indication is the necessity of installing a program in order to make the modem function. To install a traditional modem, or hardmodem, you only need to open the icon "modems" that is in Windows Control Panel, and search. The modem can function without problems without installing any drivers. You should create only an INF file (a small text file with the configurations and specifications of the modem) in order that it is recognized correctly. A softmodem will only function with it's emulator program installed.

A visual inspection helps because a softmodem has many less components that a conventional modem. Modern motherboards have on-board modems also, that also, obviously, work using software.

As always you get what you pay for. Do you pay more for a higher quality component or less for an inferior one. If you are assembling a top of the line computer it would not be a good idea to save a few dollars on the modem, but if you are working at the bottom end of the market with low cost computers, then a softmodem is a good way to cut costs, as we have seen, the difference can be as much as 60 dollars. Personally, I would prefer to invest in a 33.6K hardmodem that costs approximately the same as a 56K.

PRINTERS

As the name itself suggests, a printer is a device that is destined to print text or images, on paper or some other medium. The difference between the innumerous printer models is how the printing is achieved.

There are actually four basic types of printers: dot matrix, wich are rapidly losing ground, ink jet, laser, and thermal printers as used in fax machines. Each kind of printer operates with different technologies to obtain a printed impression.

Dot Matrix Printers

Dot matrix printers use a set of print needles, usually 9, that hit against the paper through an ink ribbon thus leaving marks on the paper. Dot matrix printers are much more economical than ink jet or laser printers because a ribbon is very cheap and may be used for a long time. A ribbon for an Epson LX 300, for example costs less than $2 and may print hundreds of pages.

Even with the popularity of ink jet printers, dot matrix printers continue to be used in some areas, due to their low printing cost, durability and principally due to their capacity to print several carbon copies at the same time.

Ink Jet printers

Ink jet printers are the printers that are most sold at the moment. Instead of using a ribbon and needles like a dot matrix printer, ink jet printers work by spraying small jets of ink onto the paper, thus managing a good quality impression, close to that of a laser printer. Another advantage of these printers is their low cost, wich makes them perfect for domestic use.

Ink jet printers basically use two types of printing technology: bubble jet, and piezoelectric.

Bubble Jet technology was created by Canon, who still have the patent. This technology involves heating the ink with a small heating element thus forming air bubbles that spray the ink violently against the paper. This technology is used in various models of printers, such as Canon and HP.

A disadvantage of this technology is that due to heating up, the print heads wear out after a short time, thus losing their precision. However, because they are extremely simple they are cheap to make and for this reason are built into the print cartridges.

Epson printers use another technology with a **Piezoelectric** print head that functions more or less like a microscopic pump spreading the ink on the paper. The print head consists of a small tube with a piezoelectric crystal close to the end. When it is electrified this crystal vibrates expelling small drops of ink from the cartridge.

As Piezoelectric print heads have a greater durability and are much more complicated and expensive than bubble jets, they are not changed together with the cartridges, but are part of the printer itself. On one hand this is good because it helps to lower the cartridges costs, but on the other it leaves the printer more susceptible to problems, like blocked print head that sometimes results in expensive service that may be half the cost of a new printer

Reconditioned cartridges

Original cartridges such as those of HP, Epson and others, have a relatively high price. As it is possible to refill the cartridge, it is customary to find reconditioned cartridges for sale at less than one third the price of a new cartridge.

Many people think that these cartridges are not worth it because they say they can damage the printer. But the cartridges may cause damage to printers only when the printer has fixed print heads such as in Epson printers. In this case a refill cartridge of low quality may block the print heads, rendering the printer almost unusable, and costing almost half the price of a new printer to change the print heads.

This danger doesn't exist for HP or other ink jet models because the print heads are built in to the disposable cartridge, the most that can happen is that the cartridge won't function properly and you will lose your money.

A problem with these cartridges is that the print heads are not designed to work for ever. The heads begin to be worn after the second or third refill and each time the print quality is worse

In any case, taking into account the cost of reconditioned cartridges, it is a good business, at least for ink jet printers such as HP, seeing as with the cost of a new cartridge it is possible to buy three or even four reconditioned cartridges, even if you yourself don't decide to refill them at home using one of the several refill kits that are to be found on sale.

Laser Printers

In a laser printer, the image to be printed is first formed on a cylinder or mold. A laser beam generates an electrostatic charge on various parts of the cylinder. When passed over the toner reservoir the charged parts attract the toner, forming a perfect copy of the image to be printed. Then the cylinder is heated and passed over the paper transferring the toner to the paper, creating the printed image. As well as monochrome laser printers, there are colored laser printers that use four colors to obtain perfect images.

Laser printers offer a much superior print quality as well as being much faster. The biggest obstacle to their mass acceptance, however, is their high cost. While an ink jet printer may be acquired for much less than 200 dollars the simplest lasers cost at least 500 to 800 dollars. And this is only for a monochrome printer, colored models are several times these prices

SCANNERS

Scanners function in a very simple manner, limited to transforming scanned images into digital signals that may be understood by the computer. To manage this miracle, the scanner uses photoelectric cells to transform the image into a series of small dots, each one with its own color, thus forming a bitmap.

As in all analogue-digital conversions there is always a small loss in quality from the original. How much is lost in terms of quality depends entirely on the supported resolutions and the number of colors recognized by the scanner.

The most commonly sold are desktop scanners with a resolution of 300 or 600 DPI (dots per inch) and with a capacity of recognizing 16 million colors. These scanners, as long as they are correctly configured are capable of producing good quality scanned images.

Nowadays practically all scanners are connected to the parallel port of the computer wich greatly simplifies their installation. In this case the printer is daisy chained to the scanner. Sharing the same parallel port between the printer and the scanner does not cause any conflict except for the small inconvenience of not being able to scan an image and print at the same time. If you try to do both at the same time, the two will share the port, the printer will print a bit, pause, the scanner will scan a bit of the image, the printer will print a bit and so on.

There are also scanners that use the SCSI interface, while some older scanners used their own proprietary interfaces.

INTERPOLATION

Scanners destined to the domestic market generally have a resolution of 300 or 600 DPI. However it is customary to see advertisements for scanners of 4800, 9600 or even 19600 9600 DPI.

The real resolution of these scanners continues to be the same, 300 or 600 dots per inch. However using specific software programs we can interpolate the image, artificially increasing its resolution to 4800 or 9600 DPI. Interpolation of images consists in adding more dots to it, based on the existing ones, thus increasing the total number of dots. Let's say that we have an image, with a tone of green with a value of 100, and another with a value of 20. The software will simply calculate the average and put between the two a green dot with a tonality of 60. In case the interpolation continued, there would be another dot with a tonality of 40 between the 20 and the 60, a dot with a tonality of 80 between the 60 and the 100 and so on as in the figure below.

In practice, the interpolation serves to smear the image, only giving the impression of a greater resolution. Interpolation is generally used for small images that need to be expanded to be used. By using interpolation we avoid the image appearing too bitty, thus hiding its low resolution.

OCR

There are several programs that are capable of recognizing letters within an image transforming it into text that may be freely edited. Normally you will receive an OCR (Optical Character Recognition) program together with the scanner, but there are commercial versions with more resources

CD-ROMs, Sound Cards, Modems, Printers and Scanners

8 CHOOSE THE BEST CONFIGURATION

As we have studied up until now, all the components directly influence the global performance of the computer. As in a car, a single component with low performance affects the whole system negatively.

In spite of the desire of everyone to have a computer equipped with the very best processor, oodles of RAM memory, lots of gigabytes of hard disk space, 3D video card, DVD etc., not everybody has $2000 or $3000 available to spend on such a configuration. This is where the cost benefit ratio enters into the picture: How to determine which configuration is the best within the limits of what we have to spend. .The objective of this chapter is exactly this, to help you choose the best configuration in terms of cost benefits in each case. To do this we will study how each component affects the performance and in which applications each is most important.

The first thing that should be taken into account is what application the computer is aimed at, that is to say, what programs will be used in it.

A computer used in an Office, for example, where only Word, Excel and Internet will be used, does not need a very powerful processor, but a reasonable quantity of memory is indispensable as well as a reasonably fast hard disk. A computer destined to games however will need a fast processor combined with a good 3D video card.

CHOOSING THE MOTHERBOARD

The motherboard is the component that should be chosen with most care. A low quality motherboard will put at risk both the performance and the reliability of the computer equipment.

When buying a motherboard check which processors it supports, if it has an AGP slot and if it has sufficient ISA and PCI slots for the peripherals that you want to install.

The most important question is the quality of the motherboard. Beside the of resources, this is the principal difference among the various makes and models that you will find on the market. Low quality motherboards as well as impairing performance, may make the computer unstable, causing constant hang-ups in Windows. Hang-ups are frequently caused by hardware and not by program bugs.

Try to find motherboards manufactured by well respected names such as Asus, Abit, Soyo and Supermicro. You will also find motherboards such as Tomato, which are also reasonable and normally cost less. Intel motherboards are also excellent Many manufacturers use Intel chipsets in their motherboards, but this is not necessarily sign of quality. A poor quality motherboard will still not be worthwhile even if it has an good chipset.

You may wonder why these motherboards are inferior, especially considering that in many cases they are using the same chipsets as well known brands. The difference is in the quality of the circuit board. A motherboard is made using a technique called MPCB (multiple layer contact board) that consists of a circuit board made up with various sub layers. A circuit board like this has to be manufactured with very high precision because the smallest error in the positioning of the tracks may cause interference making the board unstable. This also impairs the performance, impeding communication between the components at normal speeds. The difference in performance between a computer with a good motherboard and another with a similar but lower quality one may be up to 20%. This would be like changing a Pentium 600 for a Pentium 500MHz!

The problems described above are a result of cutting costs, reducing development time, and using cheaper and less precise production methods.

Certainly it is very tempting to see an advertisement for a motherboard that comes with sound card, video card and modem, all for $60 or so, whilst a motherboard of a good make costs 80, 100 or even 150 dollars and generally doesn't have any of these accessories on-board. But remember that this saving may bring you lots of headaches in the form of instability, hang-ups and incompatibility. These motherboards may even be used in cheaper computers aimed at lighter applications where the cost factor is more important, but don't think of using them in a more professional computer. It will not be worth the pain. If the problem is money, I would prefer to buy a simpler processor and install it in a better motherboard.

CHOOSING THE OTHER PERIPHERALS

There are basically four factors that determine the performance of a computer: The processor, the quantity of RAM memory, the speed of the hard disk and the video card. The importance of each varies according to the application of the computer.

RAM Memory

If the computer has little RAM memory, the processor will have to use the hard disk to store data that should be stored in memory, making the system extremely slow. However installing more memory than necessary would only be a waste, because it would not make the system any faster.

You will note that more memory needs to be installed when the computer becomes slow and accesses the hard disk intermittently when it is host used.

If the user works only with light applications like Word, Excel, Internet and doesn't usually open more than one application at once, then 32 megabytes may be sufficient, although 48 would be the ideal.

However if heavier programs are used, or various programs are opened at the same time, then the minimum should be 64 and the ideal would be 128 MB. 64 megabytes is also sufficient if the micro is destined principally to games.

In case the computer is destined to image processing, video, or desktop publishing 128 Megabytes should be used. Depending on the size of the files to be processed, the ideal may rise to 192 or even 256MB.

Installation of more memory will give new life to an older micro, especially if it only has 8 or 16 megabytes. But don't overdo it, because even with lots of memory it will be difficult to run the heavier applications due to the fragility of the whole. The ideal would be 16MB in 486s and 32 or 48Mb in Pentiums or K6 up to 233Mhz.

Processor

The installation of a more modern processor doesn't always make the computer faster. In many cases adding more memory or changing the hard disk will have a greater effect As always, it depends on the application.

In case the micro is destined principally to games, it is worthwhile investing in a first class processor like the Pentium III or AMD Athlon. In case the computer is destined to image processing or desktop publishing a top class processor will help, but only if the computer has sufficient RAM memory. If money is short, it is preferable to buy a middle of the road processor like a Celeron and invest in more memory. Avoid processors like the K6-2 and Cyrix, because as we have already seen their performance is weak in games and image processing.

Finally if the micro is destined to lighter applications the ideal would be to acquire a simpler processor like the K6-2 or Cyrix 6x86 and invest the savings in more memory, a better hard disk or a better quality motherboard.

Hard Disk

The performance of the hard disk is the determining factor as to how fast programs and files can be opened. A fast hard disk helps also if the computer has little memory. Even with a super fast processor and lots of memory, everything will be slow if the hard disk can't keep up.

Almost always you will find that larger hard disks are faster, but there are always exceptions. Find out the access time, the rpm, and the disk density.

The access time of the disk generally varies from 9 to 14 milliseconds depending on the HD. The access time determines how much time the read head takes to find data. A low value signifies a better performance.

The rotation speed is measured in RPM, or revolutions per minute. The faster a disk spins, the faster data will be found. The density, or how much data fits in each disk also determines the performance, because as the data is closer together, it will be found more rapidly. You can calculate the density by dividing the total capacity of the hard disk by the number of read heads that it has (because the disk has one platter for each read head). A 6Gb disk with 4 read heads for example, has a density of 1.5 GB per disk. The greater the density the better.

Video Card

As we have seen there are as many 3D video cards as there are 2D video cards. In case the micro is destined to games, or 3D image processing (using programs like 3D studio for example), a 3D video card is indispensable otherwise the micro will simply not be able to run the application or will be extremely slow.

If it is to be used only for office applications or 2D images, a 3D video card is not necessary.

There are many 3D accelerators that should be used in conjunction with a normal 2D card (Monster 1 and Monster 2 for example), as well as Combo cards that perform both functions such as the Viper v330, Viper v550, Viper v770, ATI Rage, Monster 3, etc. Check this detail when you buy yours. If you decide to buy an accelerator card, you will also need to buy a 2D card.

Sound card

The sound card has no influence on the performance of the computer, it only determines the audio quality. For normal use a simple sound card like a Soundblaster or even a generic sound card like those with Yamaha chipsets are adequate. More expensive cards will make a difference if you are going to work with sound editing or make a question of listening to MIDI or MP3 with a maximum of quality.

There are also 3D soundcards like the Turtle Beach Montego and the Sound Blaster Live, that generate sounds that appear to come from all directions, even using normal loudspeakers. This effect is very interesting in games, because it gives a much greater sensation of realism. Imagine hearing the sound of a shot as if it had been fired by someone behind you.

Upgrades

To make an upgrade means to change some already outdated components of a computer with a view to improving performance. However many times the computer is so outdated that it would be necessary to change almost all the components in order to reach a reasonable level of performance. In this case it is better to sell the old computer and buy a new one.

The secret in making a good upgrade is to detect the weak points of the configuration, components that may have a performance significantly inferior to the rest of the computer. Here are some configurations to serve as examples:

Configuration 1: Pentium 233 MMX

32 MB memory

HD 2.6 GB

Vídeo card 2 MB

Monitor SVGA 14"

Now we have a balanced configuration. The only viable changes would be to increase the memory to 64 MB, in case 32 MB are not enough for the use it is being put to, or change the hard disk if the user is running out of space.

It would not be a good idea to think about changing the processor because to install a Pentium, Celeron or even a K6-2 we would also have to change the motherboard. If the memory modules were of 72 pins, the cost would be greater, because modern motherboards only use sockets with 168 pins

In case the user likes games, or wants to work with 3 D images then a simple 3D video card would be a good Idea.

Configuration 2: Pentium II 266 MHz

64 MB memory

HD 2.2 GB

Vídeo card 2 MB

Monitor SVGA 15"

The first thing to consider in this example would be to change the processor for a Celeron of 433 or 466 MHz, if it is possible to change only the processor. Then we would have an excellent configuration with the exception of the hard disk which is very small and relatively slow for a computer of this size. It would be good to change it for one of 8Gb or even 13GB.

If we were to add a 3D video card we would then have almost a first class computer.

Increasing the memory to 128 MB should only be considered if the computer is being used for desktop publishing etc.

9   Assembling and Configuring

Assembling and configuring a computer is much easier than it appears at first sight. It may be summed up in installing and screwing the components and configuring some jumpers on the motherboard. After the computer has been assembled and functioning comes the most difficult part, that of installing the operating system and configuring the system, which we will look at in the next few chapters.

The first thing that you should know about and how to avoid it is static electricity. Static electricity is generated by friction and is easily built up on our body, especially in dry places. You may have seen or experienced it when you walked on a woolen carpet and touched a door knob and received a shock, or something similar. Computer components are quite susceptible to electric charges and may be easily damaged by a small shock like this.

When handling hardware in is extremely advisable to take certain precautions to avoid accidents. The first is that when handling expansion cards or memory modules, hold them by the edges avoiding direct contact with the chips and principally with any metallic contacts. In this way, even if you know that you are electrically charged it is difficult to cause any damage, as the printed circuit board fiberglass is an isolating material.

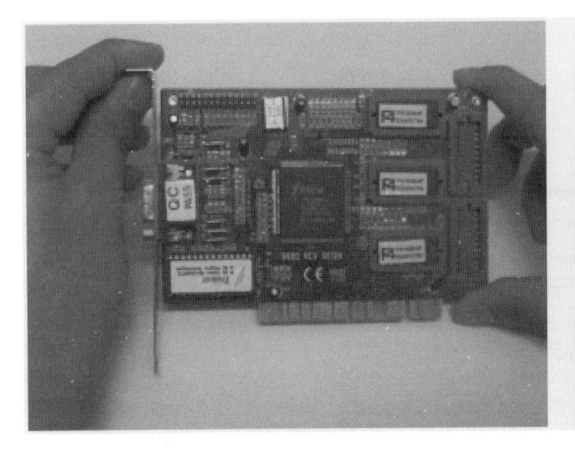

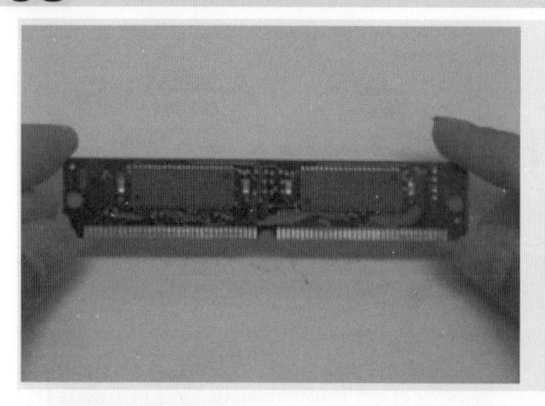

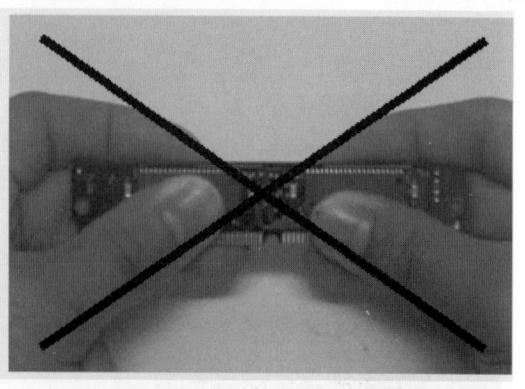

Another precaution is not to use any woolen clothes, jerseys etc, because these are excellent attractors of static electricity just by the movement of the body. Also avoid handling components in carpeted areas especially if you are without shoes. It is also recommended to discharge any accumulated static electricity before touching any components, by touching on any metal piece that is earthed, such as a metal water pipe or unpainted metal windows frames or grills.

Another solution is to use an antistatic grounding strap that may be easily acquired in most computer shops. This strap has a wire that should be connected to an earth, thus eliminating any electrical charge from the body. If you don't have any metal that is earthed or an antistatic strap, a less efficient manner of discharging static is by simply touching on the power supply Box or any other unpainted metal part of the computer cabinet for a few seconds.

Contrary to what it may appear, damage to components by the static electricity of our body is not as common as you might think, because we don't normally accumulate large static electricity charges on our bodies. You don't need to be frightened of touching any computer components thinking that you are going to damage them with static electricity, but it is always wise to take precautions, better safe than sorry, and always handle the boards by their edges.

BEGINNING THE ASSEMBLY

At the moment motherboards that use AT style cases and others that use ATX ones are to be found. Although the assembly in both cases involves basically the same processes, there are a few differences that need to be analyzed. To make things easier, I shall first describe the assembly process using an AT motherboard and a mini tower case and then I will just explain what changes when we use an ATX motherboard and case.

Not many tools are needed to assemble a computer. A Phillips screwdriver and another ordinary one are about all you need. Some other tools like nut drivers, tweezers, long nose pliers, and some heat conducting grease are also useful sometimes. Any necessary screws will come with the case, motherboard and other components.

Assembling and Configuring 99

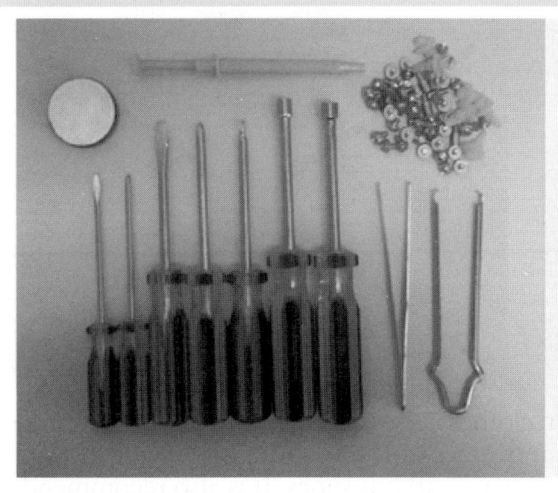

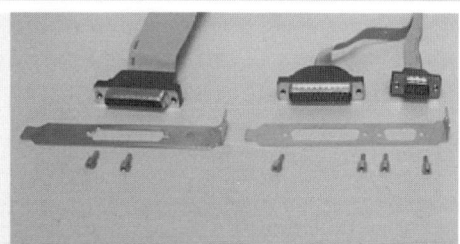

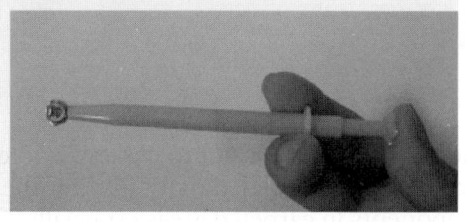

We may use the nut drivers to remove or tighten the majority of screws especially those that fix the serial and parallel port sockets to their mounting plates that can only be removed with these or pliers. A Phillips screwdriver, or a nut driver may be used for the screws like those that fix the cover and circuit boards. Tweezers are very useful for changing jumpers in areas that are difficult to access.

Now that we have seen some of the tools to be used, how about beginning to assemble our computer? In the photo you can see all the components that we are going to use: mini tower case, motherboard, processor, memory, video card, sound card, CD-ROM, diskette drive and the cables and screws.

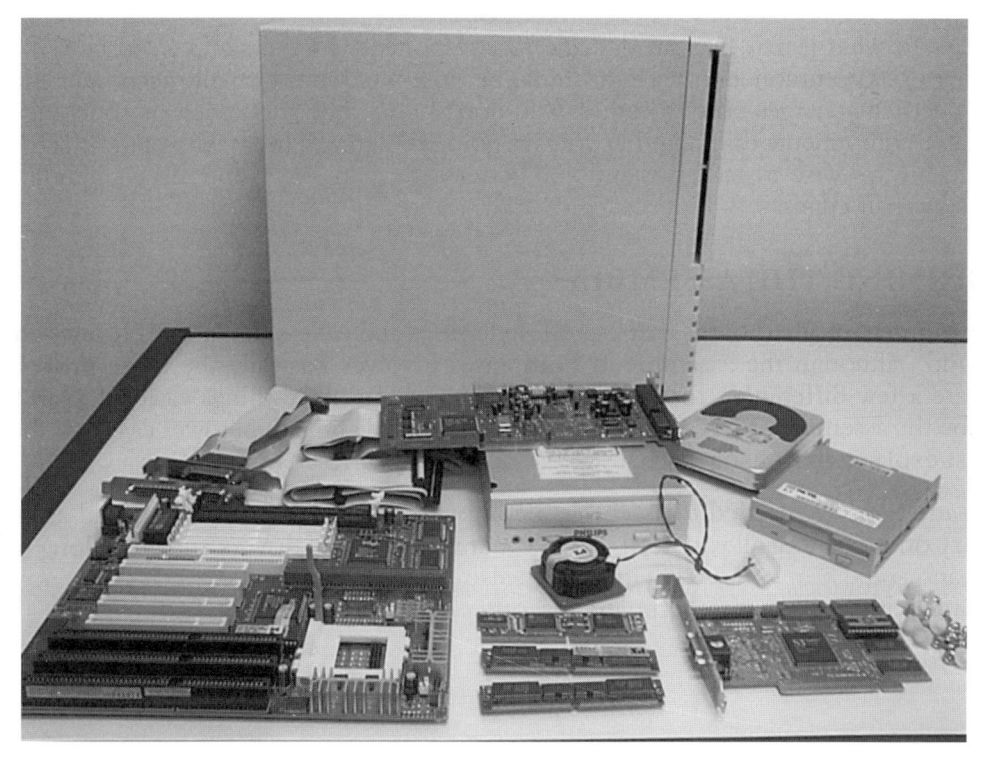

HARDWARE PC

To begin assembly, the first thing to do is unscrew and remove the base plate where the motherboard is going to be mounted. After fixing the motherboard to its base plate, we can install several other things before putting the motherboard etc back into the cabinet. It is easier to install the memory, processor, some cables and to change jumpers with the motherboard out of the cabinet.

To fix the motherboard to the mounting plate we use plastic spacers as well as one or two hexagonal brass spacers. The spacers are plastic pieces rather like a large drawing pin. The pointed end should be placed in the corresponding holes in the motherboard, whilst the base will fit into the cutouts on the mounting plate.

The motherboard would not be very well secured if we only used the plastic spacers. To fix it more firmly we use the hexagonal brass spacers. This is screwed firmly to the base plate and the motherboard is fastened to it with a second small screw. Generally two of these are sufficient together with the plastic spacers to secure the motherboard firmly.

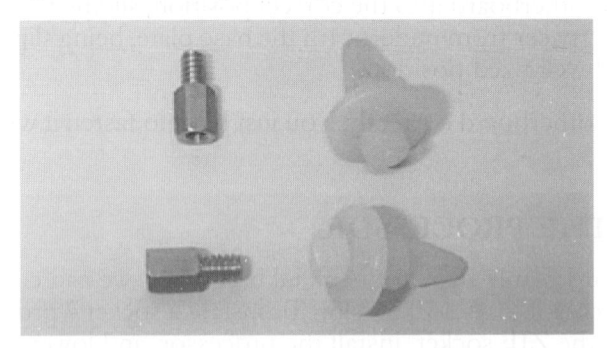

Hexagonal brass spacers beside of plastic spacers (White).

To fix the motherboard to its base plate is one of the most complicated parts of the assembly process. The first step is to examine the mother board and the base plate to see which holes for the spacers match up. Sometimes to give better support for the motherboard, you can cut the lower part of the plastic spaces using a knife, scissors etc, and place them in holes in the motherboard where there is no counterpart on the metal base plate.

Te first step to fix the motherboard to the base plate is to see where the holes in both match up. (**1**)

Now you should fix the hexagonal brass spacers into the metal base plate in the places where there is a corresponding hole in the motherboard (**2**) and fit the other plastic spacers into the motherboard (**3**).

Now just place the motherboard into the correct position, sliding it a little if necessary. In photo 4 we can see a spacer from underneath the base plate, being slipped into its slot, and in the detail, its final well fixed position.

Having placed the motherboard correctly, you just have to fasten it with a couple of small Phillips screws.(**5**)

INSTALLING THE PROCESSOR

With the motherboard firmly fixed to its metal base plate, we can continue the assembly by installing the processor in its socket/slot. To install a socket 7 processor raise the little lever on the side of the ZIF socket, install the processor, and lower the lever that should snap into place. Don't worry about installing the processor the wrong way, because on e of the corners as one less pin, and may be chamfered, and can only be installed in one way.

Chamfer where there is one less pin on the processor and the ZIF socket.

The processor should fit easily into the socket. If there is any resistance see if there are any bent pins. If there are, you may try to straighten them using a small screwdriver, or other metal object, or even your fingernails, taking care however to discharge any static electricity first, and especial care not to break the pin, or the processor will be rendered unusable.

To cool the processor while in use, a cooling fan should be placed above it. Coolers are normally fixed to the socket using a metal spring clip as in the photo. In case your processor is "boxed" you don't need to worry about installing a cooler because it comes together with the processor. Don't forget to connect the power cable of the cooler to a suitable connector also.

Cooler clamped above a processor using a metal spring clip fixed to the ZIF socket.

Slotting a Pentium II or III

Unlike from the other processors that use the socket 7 or similar, the Pentium II, III, and Celeron use a different kind of socket, baptized by Intel as Slot One. Although the socketing of the processor is a little more laborious, it is not more difficult, just needing a little more patience.

The first step is to install the plastic supports that serve to help secure the processor in place. These supports are necessary for the Pentium II because of its metal encapsulation and the cooler it is very heavy and may shift with movement of the case, causing bad contacts. As well as the main support that is screwed to slot one, a second support may be used being fixed into the holes in the front of it. The function of this second support is to serve as a support for the cooler fixing the whole more firmly in place. In the case of the Celeron, we use only the cooler support because this processor does not have the meta

Plastic supports used by the Pentium II

The support for the Pentium II is fixed to the two holes in the motherboard using plastic pins with self locking caps. To fix the support, remove the caps, place the support and put back the self locking caps which should keep in securely in place.

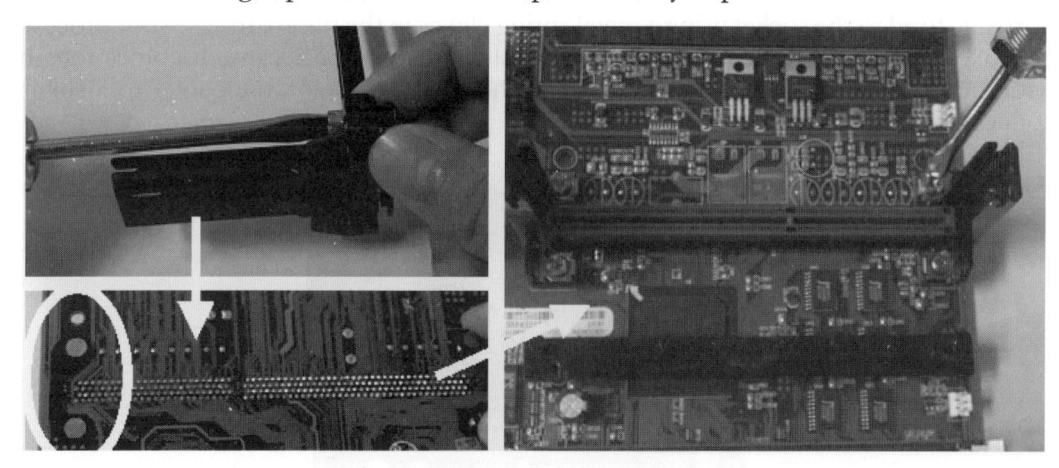

To affix the Pentium II support to the motherboard, first free the two pins, fixing them in the four holes to the side of the Slot 1and screw them to the main base. At the same time the cooler support can be installed.

After fixing the supports to the motherboard, you just have to slot in the Pentium processor like a video game cartridge. Don't worry about slotting it in the wrong way round as there are keyways in slot one that only permit it to be installed one way round. Don't forget also to plug the cooler power cable into the 3 pin socket at the side of slot one.

104 HARDWARE PC

The Celeron is slotted in the same way as the Pentium. Don't forget to use the plastic supports so that the processor cannot become loose, causing bad contacts.

Removing a Pentium II processor is a little more complicated because you need to squeeze the locking latches at the sides at the same time as you remove it. You can use the index fingers to push the latches while you hold the processor with the thumbs. In case of any difficulties, ask a friend to help.

FITTING THE MEMORY MODULES

Fitting memory modules is a fairly simple operation. To install a 30 or 72 pin module, place it in the socket inclined at an angle of about 45° and push it until it clicks into place.

To avoid installing the module the wrong way round, check the cutout at one end of the module wich should correspond to a key in one side of the socket.

In some cases of low quality motherboards you may find some resistance when pushing the memory module. Don't attempt to force it or you will damage the socket. In this case hold both locking springs open with your thumbs while you push the module with your fingers.

Putting 168 pin modules into their slots is also simple. Free the plastic locks at each end of the socket and place the memory into the slot, like a video game cartridge. Press firmly on both ends with the thumbs and it should snap into place. The plastic locks will close also, press these to close them completely and you will know then that it is fixed properly in place. If you prefer, you can also possible to click one side into place first, and then the other.

FITTING COAST MODULES

As we saw in the chapter about motherboards, some older boards didn't have any L2 cache memory at all, they just had a socket where a COAST (Cache on a Stick) memory module could be installed instead, usually with 256 or 512 Kbytes.

Nowadays no motherboards have these sockets, but if you are going to deal with slightly older computers, you will run across these now and then.

Fitting a COAST is as simple as a normal memory module, just fit it in the socket as with the others. There are keyways to avoid it being fitted the wrong way round.

Don't worry if you have to use a little bit of force, this is normal with COAST modules. To remove it pull each side alternately with a little force, or use a screwdriver as a lever.

106   HARDWARE PC

JUMPER CONFIGURATION

Motherboards usually offer support for various processors. In a slightly older motherboard equipped with the chipsets i430FX, i430VX, i430TX, i430HX or other manufacturers equivalents, you can usually install a Pentium from 75 MHz up to a 233 MMX, just by configuring the jumpers on the motherboard correctly.

As we have seen, jumpers are small pieces of plastic with a metal contact inside that links two jumper pins on the motherboard. By positioning the jumpers we can tell the motherboard how it should operate. Setting the jumpers is the part of the assembly that requires the greatest attention, if they are not set right the computer will not function properly, i may not even switch on, and in extreme cases you can even damage components. (By setting a much higher than normal voltage for the processor for example).

To know the correct jumper settings you will have to consult the manual for the motherboard

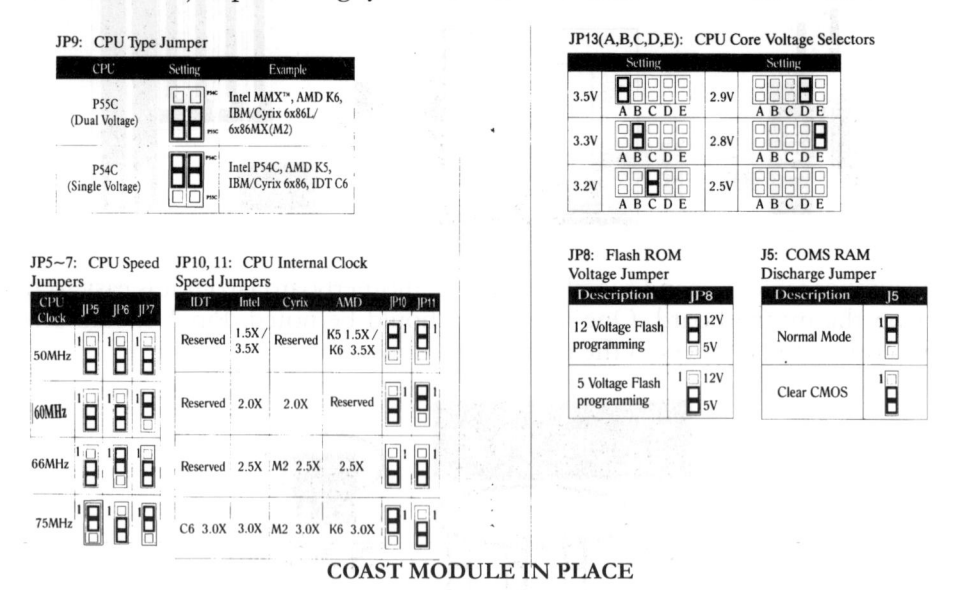

COAST MODULE IN PLACE

Note that each jumper is numbered, like JP8, JP13, etc. These numbers serve as a reference to help find the jumpers on the motherboard.

As well as tables that have information on the positioning and settings of the jumpers, you

Assembling and Configuring

will find a layout diagram that indicates the position of each jumper on the motherboard. These diagrams not only show jumper positions but also identify the various serial, parallel sockets, IDE interfaces etc. as well as the connectors for the front panel, power, etc

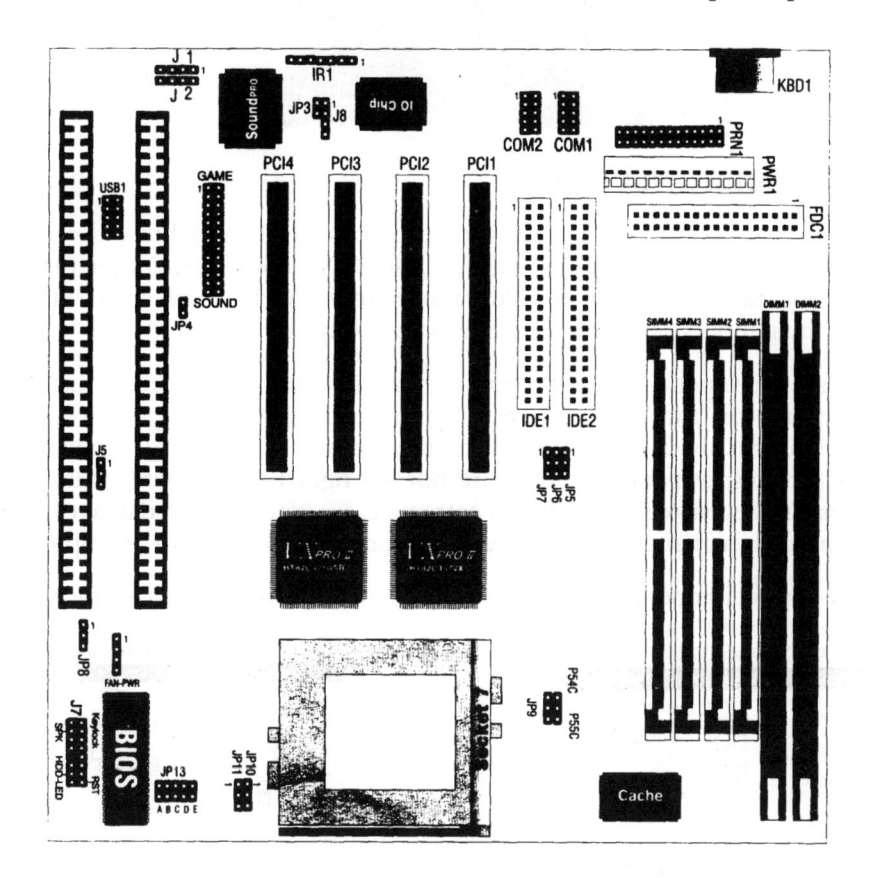

With the jumper tables at hand together with the motherboard layout it is easy to find the jumpers on the motherboard. One last thing should be noted. Pin 1 should always be marked to orient the jumpers in the correct positions.

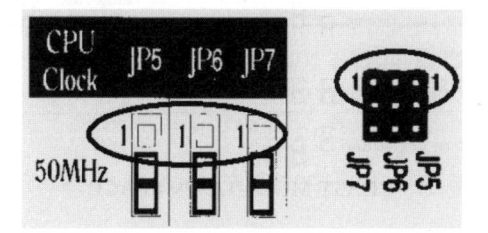

The position of pin 1should be the same in the jumper layout and the motherboard to ensure correct orientation of the jumpers.

Now that we have found the jumpers necessary to configure the motherboard let see how this is done.

PROCESSOR SPEED

Modern processors use a resource called clock multiplier. This means that the processor functions internally at a greater speed than the motherboard. A Pentium 200 for example, even though it functions internally at 200 MHz, communicates with the motherboard at only 66 MHz. The speed at which the processor operates is called the internal clock speed whilst that of the motherboard is called the external clock speed.

Continuing with the Pentium 200 as an example, we can see that the internal processor speed of 200 MHz is 3 times greater than the motherboard (66 MHz), so we say that the Pentium 200 has a multiplier of 3X. In a Pentium 166 the multiplier will be 2.5X as the processor frequency of 166 MHz is 2.5 times the external (motherboard) frequency of 66 MHz.

In micros equipped with Pentium or similar processors the clock frequency of the motherboard may be configured as 50 MHz, 60 MHz, 66 MHz and depending on the motherboard may also be 55 MHz, 75 MHz and 83 MHz. More recent motherboards operate at 100 MHz and there are some that operate at or will soon operate at 103, 112, 120 133MHz, and more.

Sometimes it is possible to configure a processor in two different ways. A Pentium 100 for example may be configured with an external clock of 50 MHz and a multiplier of 2X or an external clock of 66 MHz with a multiplier of 1.5X. In this case the second option is recommended because even though the processor continues functioning at the same frequency, the other components will be functioning 33% faster, significantly the overall performance of the equipment.

Some slightly older motherboards only support multipliers up to 3X, however we can put the jumper to 1.5X when installing a 233 MMX. This happens because the processor recognizes a multiplier of 1.5X as 3.5 with the objective of maintaining compatibility with older boards. Similar processors such as the K6 of 233 MHz also take advantage of this.

Although Intel abandoned the manufacture of the Pentium MMX after the 233 MHz version, manufacturing only the Pentium II that uses boards equipped with a slot One, Cyrix and AMD continued to launch socket 7 processors with faster clocks. To use some of these processors you will need a motherboard with a super 7 socket, that supports multipliers greater than 3 and maybe a BUS of 100 MHz.

Below is a table showing the multipliers and external clock frequencies for various processors.

Assembling and Configuring

Processor	Internal clock	Multiplier	External Clock
Pentium	75 MHz	1.5x	50 MHz
	100 MHz	1.5x	66 MHz
	120 MHz	2x	60 MHz
	133 MHz	2x	66 MHz
	150 MHz	2.5x	60 MHz
	166 MHz	2.5x	66 MHz
	200 MHz	3x	66 MHz
Pentium MMX	166 MHz	2.5x	66 MHz
	200 MHz	3x	66 MHz
	233 MHz	3.5x (configured as 1.5x)	66 MHz
Pentium II	233 MHz	3,5x	66 MHz
	266 MHz	4x	66 MHz
	300 MHz	4.5x or 3x	66 MHz or 100MHz
	333 MHz	5x	66 MHz
	350 MHz	3.5	100 MHz
	400 MHz	4x	100 MHz
	450 MHz	4.5x	100 MHz
AMD K6	166 MHz	2.5x	66 MHz
	200 MHz	3x	66 MHz
	233 MHz	3.5x (configured as 1.5x)	66 MHz
	266 MHz	4x	66 MHz
	300 MHz	4.5 or 3x	66 MHz or 100 MHz
AMD K6-2	300 MHz	4.5x or 3x	66 MHz or 100 MHz
	350 MHz	3.5x	100 MHz
	400 MHz	4x	100 MHz

Cyrix processors are an exception to the rule because they are not sold according to their operating frequency but according to an index created by Cyrix called the Pr rating, wich compares its performance to a Pentium processor. A Cyrix 6x86 MX Pr 233, for example, operates at only 187 MHz using a multiplier of 2.5x and an external clock of 75MHz, There are also versions that operate at 200 MHz, using a multiplier of 3x and an external clock of 66 MHz.

Processor	Internal Clock	Multiplier	External Clock
6x86 MX Pr 166	133 ou 150 MHz	2x ou 2.5x	66 ou 60 MHz
6x86 MX Pr 200	166 MHz	2.5x	166
6x86 MX Pr 233	187 ou 200 MHz	2.5x ou 3x	75 ou 66 MHz
6x86 MX Pr 266	225 ou 233 MHz	3x ou 3.5x	75 ou 66 MHz
6x86 MII Pr 300	225 ou 233 MHz	3x ou 3.5x	75 ou 66 MHz
6x86 MII Pr 333	250 MHz	2.5x	100 MHz
6x86 MII Pr 350	300 MHz	3x	100 MHz

In the case of the Pentium II many motherboards are capable of automatically detecting the operating speed of the processor. These motherboards are called jumperless because they don't have any jumpers, all configuration is done through the SETUP. In others there is only a set of jumpers that directly defines the processor speed. So much so, as that in position X the processor will operate ate 266 MHz and with setting Y the processor will operate at 300 MHz for example.

WHAT IS OVERCLOCKING?

Unlike what most people think, the processors operating speeds are not defined by them, but by the motherboard.

In the motherboard there is a small quartz crystal called a clock generator, that oscillates at millions of cycles per second with almost perfect precision. The vibrations of this crystal are used to synchronize the motherboard cycles that knows with each vibration of the crystal it should generate a certain number of cycles.

It is more or less like a traffic light that opens and closes several times per minute. When the light is closed the traffic stops, and when it is opened the traffic flows. A clock pulse is just light, a green light that makes all the peripherals work simultaneously and in synchronization. The functioning of all peripherals from the video card to the hard disk are controlled by this clock.

Processors don't have a clock generator and for this reason work using the signal received from the motherboard. In a 200MHz Pentium for example, the motherboard functions at 66 MHz, and the multiplier is 3x which signifies for each motherboard cycle, the processor will generate 3 cycles.

Exactly because the processor is limited to the frequency of the motherboard (Or multiple thereof), its frequency is not fixed, and may be greater or less than specified. Rather like an electric motor that has an ideal speed, but may turn faster or slower with a little adjustment.

In order to maintain compatibility with various processors, current motherboards may operate at different frequencies and therefore we can sometimes make the processor work faster than normal simply by configuring the motherboard to work at a higher frequency. This technique is called overclocking.

For example, a Pentium 120 works with a motherboard functioning at 60 MHz and with a multiplier of 2x. If we configured the motherboard to work at 66 MHz and kept the multiplier at 2x the processor would then work at 133 MHz. If the motherboard frequency was increased to 75 MHz the processor would function at 150 MHz. There is no magic to this, you just need to alter the jumpers on the motherboard. Read the manual to see what the possibilities are. In some more modern motherboards, the bus frequency is not set through jumpers, but by using the SETUP.

In many cases the processor also accepts a higher multiplier. An AMD K6 of 266 MHz, for example, works with a motherboard bus frequency of 66 MHz and with a multiplier of 4x. If we increased the multiplier to 4.5x, while keeping the motherboard functioning at 66 MHz, we would make the processor function at 300 MHz.

The performance of an overclocked processor is identical to a normal processor functioning at this speed. A Pentium 120 overclocked at 133 MHz presents the same performance as a genuine Pentium 133.

When a manufacturer develops a processor design it is tested at various different frequencies to determine its ideal operating frequency. The manufacturers generally adopt a certain safety margin and rate the processor with a frequency well below its limit. It is exactly this safety margin that permits overclocking, we are simply making the processor work at its maximum speed. This margin varies from manufacturer to manufacturer and from processor to processor. Some processors accept overclocks more than others for this reason. There are cases of processors that work without any problems with a frequency 50% greater than the original, as well as cases where the processor presents instability problems at only 10% above its rated speed.

Obviously there are some drawbacks to overclocking. By forcing it to work at a higher frequency than normal it may hangup sometimes, it can overheat, and its working life may be reduced. There is, however, no chance of damaging the processor by changing the operating frequencies or multipliers, unless the voltage is increased too much. The working life of the processor is reduced proportionally to the temperature increase. The ideal working temperature for a processor is +-40°C. and that should rend a working life of approximately 20 years. At 50°C the working life would fall to only 8 or 10 years. And above 60°C the processor would hardly reach three years. There is no possibility of burning out the processor even if the temperature reaches a critical level because the processors have a security system, a type of thermostat that switches off the processor if a certain temperature is reached thus avoiding burning it out. The temperature limit is determined by the manufacturer and varies from processor to processor, but is generally between 70 and 80° C.

Overclocking is used a lot by researchers to extract the maximum possible from their computers, or to give a bit of extra life to an already obsolete PC.

The multilpier is locked in Intel processors, and it is only possible to overclock by increasing the bus frequency. With AMD processors it is possible to overclock by increasing either or both the bus frequency or the multiplier. It is also possible to overclock Cyrix processors, but the chances are much less with these as they are already working close to their limits, having a much smaller tolerance margin.

Here are some examples below.:

112 HARDWARE PC

Processor	Overclock possibilities (Maximum)	Multiplier and bus frequency	Chances of success
Celeron 300	450 MHz	4.5x 100	80%
Celeron 366	550 MHz (!!)	5,5x 100	50% (need very good cooling)
Pentium MMX 200	249 MHz	3x 83	75%
Pentium II 400	448 MHz	4x 112	70%
Pentium III 450	600 MHz	4x 133 MHz	50% (need a very good BX board and PC-133 memory)
Celeron 266	400 MHz	4x 100	80%
Pentium II 333 MHz	375 MHz	5x 75	40%
Pentium MMX 233 MHz	261 MHz	3.5x 75	75%

If a very high frequency is chosen, whether for the processor or the motherboard, the motherboard simply won't switch on, or hangs up during initialization. There are cases where it is simply not possible to overclock, for example if the processor is a 400MHz Celeron and the motherboard only permits frequencies of 66 and 100 MHz we cannot do anything because 66 MHz is the normal operating frequency and a frequency of 100Mhz cannot be used because it will never function at 600 MHz.

It is you who decide if it is worth the trouble to overclock. Use your common sense. Begin with small increments and never increase the processor voltage.

PROCESSOR VOLTAGE

Because they are produced using different manufacturing techniques (and the constantly attempting to reduce heat and energy usage) different processors need different voltages to function correctly. As always, in order to maintain compatibility with the greatest possible number of processors, motherboards offer a choice of voltages which may be chosen through the use of jumpers.

To set the voltage higher than specified for the processor will cause overheating wich in some cases may damage the processor or in extreme cases render it useless. If the voltage is not sufficient, the processor will be unstable, or not function.

The motherboard manual contains specifications of the voltages and the jumper settings for each.

Pentium classic (P54C) voltages

There are two types of Pentium processors, that even though they have identical performance, use entirely different manufacturing techniques and for this reason operate at different voltages. VRE processors use 3.5V whilst STD models use 3.3 V.

To know if your Pentium is VRE or STD look at the lower part of it as shown below. There are various data written here about the processor. In the third line for example, "A80502133" you can see that the last three digits indicate the processor speed, in this case a Pentium 133. In the 4th line SY022/SSS, the first letter after the slash represents what type of processor it is. If it is "**S**" then it is an STD processor, and if it is a "**V**" we are dealing with a VRE processor. In this case there is an SSS after the slash that indicates the processor shown in the photo is STD.

Many motherboards only offer 3.5 volts and don't supply the ideal 3.3V for STD processors, bur you can set the voltage 3.5 volts and use it in these motherboards. Theoretically this voltage increase would cause an increase in the working temperature of the processor because it is not the ideal one for its normal operation. In practice however this configuration will not cause damage and may be used without problems.

Pentium MMX (P55C) voltages

The Pentium MMX uses a voltage of 2.8 V. Actually, this voltage is only used by the core, or nucleus of the processor. The circuits the processor uses to communicate with the outside world like the chipset etc, continue functioning at 3.3 volts the same as the Pentium STD. For this we say that the MMX is dual voltage.

As the MMX instructions are only software, this processor does not need any special support on behalf of the motherboard. Any motherboard offering support for the Pentium 200 will also support the MMX 166, 200 processors, and also the 233 MHz version, which can be configured in this case with a multiplier of 1.5x. The only problem is the voltage. Not all older motherboards offer the dual voltage support required by the MMX, wich may impede us from using them in conjunction with these processors.

Once more it is necessary to check in the manual if the motherboard offers the 2.8 volts needed by MMX and which jumper needs to be set. In case your motherboard does not offer support for 2,8 V you can risk installing the MMX using 3.3 V. This is not recommendable, however, because with the higher voltage the processor will heat up more than normal reducing its working life and may even cause damage in the short term. Even so, if you are willing to try it, bear in mind that this is a risky process and as well as overheating, may damage the processor in the short term.

AMD K6 Voltages

Luckily K6 processors have the voltage stamped on the upper part of them otherwise it would be quite difficult to determine the correct voltage used by a processor of this series. AMD used two entirely different production techniques called ALR and ANR with the first versions of the K6. ALR processors use a voltage of 2.9 volts (in case the motherboard does not have this you can use 2.8V without problems), whilst ANR uses 3.2 volts (if this

114 HARDWARE PC

is not available you can also use 3.3V without problems). The APR processors using 3.3 volts were also launched later on.

Just to make things more complicated, the most recent versions of the K6 used transistors with 0.25 microns and a voltage of 2.2V. For this there is no fixed rule for K6 voltages. When you are installing one of these processors you should read the inscriptions on the upper part of the processor to know what voltage may be safely used.

Happily this confused state of affairs does not apply to the K6-2 and K6-3 processors, wich invariably use 2.2V This detail should be Taken into account when buying a motherboard for use with this processor, as not all motherboards offer this voltage.

Cyrix Voltages

All the Cyrix 6x86MX or 6x86MII processors use a voltage of 2.9V but as Cyrix themselves say, they may be used with a voltage of 2,8V without problem, in case the motherboard does not offer the ideal voltage. The exceptions are the older Cyrix 6x86 processors (prior to the 6x86MX and 6x86MII) without MMX instructions. It does not make any difference with these older processors if you use 2.9 V or 3.3 or even 3,5 volts. However, as in the case of AMD Cyrix processors they have the working voltage stamped on their upper side wich avoids any confusion.

Pentium II Voltage

Unlike to the socket 7 processors, there is no need to configure the voltage for use with a Pentium II processor. This happens because the processor is capable of signaling to the motherboard what voltage it uses, dispensing any external configuration. Many motherboards are also capable of detecting the operating speed of the Pentium II processor, dispensing any need for jumper configuration.

Just to satisfy your curiosity, the Pentium II processors based on the Klamath architecture (up to 333 MHz) use 2.8V and those based on the Deschutes (350 MHz upwards, and some of the 300 and 333 MHz ones) use 2,0 V.

OTHER CONFIGURATIONS

As well as the operating speed and the voltage used by the processor, the motherboard jumpers also permit other important resources to be configured, wich should be revised before switching the computer on.

CPU Type Jumper

Many older motherboards have a jumper called "CPU Type Jumper" wich may be configured as P55C or P54C. This jumper serves to inform the motherboard if we are using a single voltage processor (Pentium, K5, 6x86 without MMX instructions and IDT6) or one that uses dual voltage (Pentium MMX, K6, K6-2, 6x86L, 6x86MX and 6x86MII). More recent motherboards are capable of automatically detecting what type of processor is installed, and therefore don't have this jumper.

CMOS Discharge Jumper (clean CMOS)

The Setup configuration is recorded in a special memory called CMOS wich consists of a small quantity of volatile memory, fed by a small battery wich maintains the data stored.

Let's say, for example, that someone put a password in the Setup of your computer and now, as you don't know the password, you can no longer enter into your computer. A simple solution would be to erase all data from the CMOS. In this way, all the Setup information including the password would be lost. The only inconvenient things is that you would have to reconfigure the whole Setup. If this is your case, then don't worry, because a little bit later on , in the chapter on CMOS Setup, you will find out all the information you need to configure the Setup.

O CMOS Discharge Jumper may be set to "Normal Mode" or to "Clear CMOS". To clear the CMOS memory, just change the jumper position for a few seconds before returning it to its original position and switching on the computer again.

One more case where this jumper is vital is the case of jumperless Pentium II motherboards. In many of these, in spite of being automatically configured, it is possible to freely alter the multiplier and the bus frequency used by the processor as well as in some cases the processor voltages, which is useful when overclocking.

There could be a problem, for example, if you configured the Setup up incorrectly and the computer would refuse to function. In this case it is necessary to clear the CMOS in order to restore the default values to the CMOS and make the computer function again. Actually, no motherboard can be truly jumperless.as at least this jumper is necessary to reset the CMOS, if necessary.

Onboard Sound and Video

Many motherboards have sound and video chips built-in that dispense with the need for separate cards. Generally however they are of low quality, and the user will often want to install separate sound or video cards.

Jumpers will be found on these motherboards that permit the on-board sound and video to be disabled thus permitting the use of separate cards, and occasionally jumpers related to their specific functions.

Front Panel connectors

The Reset button, Turbo button, Keylock, as well as the Power, Hard Disk, and Turbo LEDS found on the frontal panel of the computer case should be connected to the motherboard in order to function.

There are various wires coming from the front panel wich should be connected to the appropriate pin connectors on the motherboard.

116 HARDWARE PC

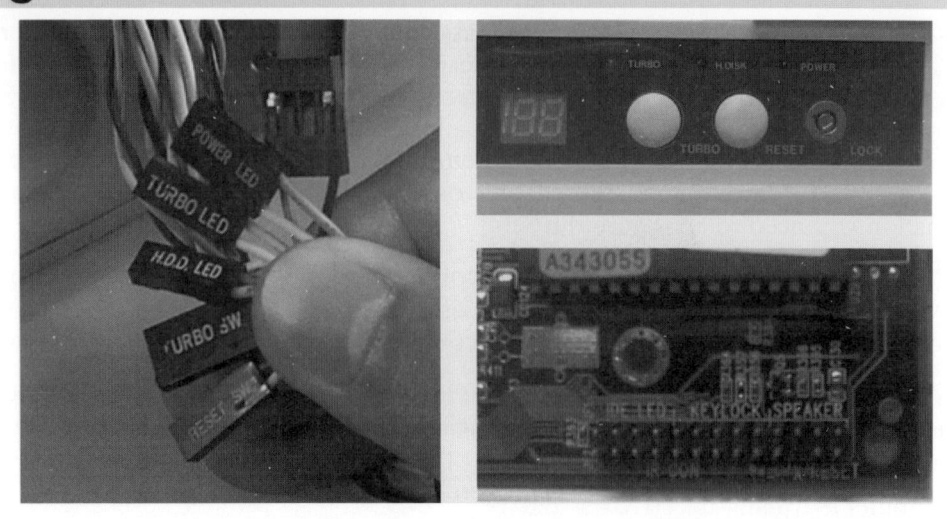

Although the motherboard always has the details printed on the circuit board to the side of these connector pins, in case you can't find one, or have any doubts, you may always refer to the manual for help. Some manuals only have a connector diagram, while others have detailed instructions on the connections.

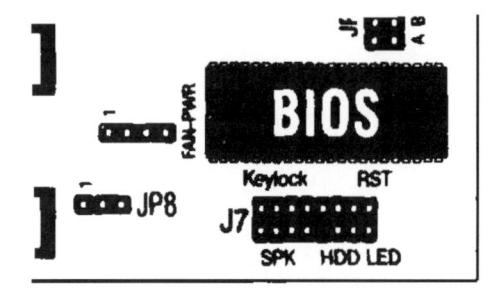

If you don't connect some of these wires it will not affect the functioning of the computer in any way, the only effects will be that the reset button, turbo switch and display LEDS will not function. They will think that you are pretty careless about assembling PCs and it will not do your reputation any good.

But enough talking, lets see to the connections:

Speaker

Even if your computer doesn't have a sound card, on many occasions you will hear some beeps. These sounds are generated directly by the processor and played through a small loudspeaker mounted in the front of the case, wich explains their low quality.

The Speaker connector has four pins, however only two wires are used, normally one red and one black, connected at the two ends of the connector. Don't worry about connecting it the wrong way round as it does not have any polarity. It just needs to be connected in the correct connector of the motherboard.

Reset

Although we can reset the computer at any moment by pressing Ctrl+Alt+Del, sometimes the computer may hang-up so badly that it can't even be reset with the keyboard. On these occasions the reset button avoids having to switch the computer off and on again.

The reset connector only has two pins with two wires, usually White and orange. This should be connected to the pins on the motherboard labeled "Reset SW", "RST", or simply "Reset". Again you don't need to worry about inverting the connections, because like the speaker there is no polarity.

Keylock

The keylock is a rudimentary manner of avoiding strangers having access to the computer. There is a lock on the front panel which when locked disables the keyboard.

Obviously this system does not offer any real protection, anybody can easily open the case and remove the wire wich is connected to the keylock switch, thus deactivating it or even open the keylock switch with a slight effort and a screwdriver or similar tool, as they are of very simple construction.

In addition, the keylock serves only to lock the keyboard and does not completely restrict access to the computer. Passwords to enter in the operating system, or at least the Setup are much more efficient.

Becouse it is of little use,one hardly finds these on sale nowadays and rarely on modern matherboards. Once again, this wire does not have any polarity, and may be connected any way round.

Hard Disk and Power LEDs

These are the little lights on the front panel that indicate if the HD is being accessed and if the computer is switched on. The Hard Disk LED, sometimes called the HDD LED, or IDE LED, is connected to the pin connector on the motherboard with the same name.

The Power LED shares the same 5 pin connector as the Keylock. Generally, the Power LED is connected to the first three and the keylock to the last two. Like in the case of the HDD LED, this connector has polarity, for this reason, if the Power light does not come on, just invert the connector.

118 HARDWARE PC

Turbo Switch and Turbo LED

Many older programs, especially prior to 1986, only functioned adequately in slow computers. This was especially true of some games from this period wich became too fast when run in a computer faster than   a 286, making them unplayable.

In order to permit that these programs could be run without problems, the turbo function was created.When pressed, it reduced the speed of the computer, making it function like at XT with a speed o 4MHz.

Obviously this key no longer has any use since no-one uses these old programs any more, and who, in right state of mind would want to make a computer slower. For this reason almost no motherboard today has a turbo switch and those with turbo switches are extremely rare.

However, you will comes across turbo connectors if you have to deal with older computers. There is no mystery about its connection, just connect the wires from the turbo button (Turbo SW or TB SW) and the LED (turbo Led, or TB Led) to the corresponding pin connectors on the motherboard.

If the wire from the turbo switch has three connectors, and the motherboard only two, just connect two of them. Connecting the turbo switch the wrong way round will only invert the operation of the button. On will be off and vice versa.

Configuring the frequency Display

Computer cases manufactured up to a short time ago possessed a small display that showed the operating frequency of the computer. This display, however, is only for appearances and may be configured to display any value, and not necessarily the true operating frequency of the processor. The display also has no effect on the functioning of the computer.

Although it has only a purely aesthetic function, the frequency display gives a lot of work in order to configure correctly, so much so that many people prefer to leave it with the factory default even if this does not correspond to the operating speed of the processor being used.

The display is nothing more than a small electric circuit that shows different numbers according to the arrangement of the jumpers on its other side. Normally the computer case comes with small piece of paper manual that explains how to set the jumpers for each desired number, but this is almost useless and few people have the patience to try to understand it.

The display is nothing more than a small electric circuit that shows different numbers according to the arrangement of the jumpers on its other side.

Assembling and Configuring **119**

If you don't have the patience to attempt to understand the manual, or even don't have one, a simple and much used method is to switch on the computer to light up the display and configure the jumpers by trial and error. People with a little bit of experience can usually do this in less than a minute.

Sometimes the display is in a difficult part of the case, to get to wich makes its configuration more difficult. In this case, you may prefer to remove the front of the case by removing the four screws that hold it, facilitating access to the display jumpers as shown below.

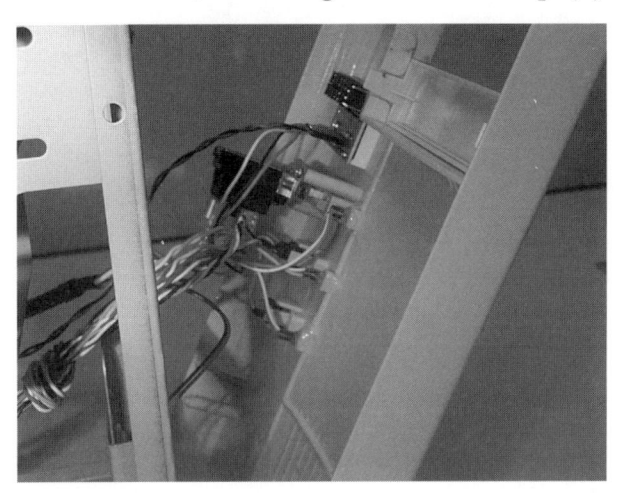

HD and CD-ROM jumpers

As well as the hard disk, sometimes other peripherals are connected to the IDE interfaces such as CD-ROMs, Zip drives, LS-120, and others.

You will find two IDE interfaces on the micro called IFDE primary and IDE secondary. Each interface permits two devices to be connected, which should be configured as Master and Slave respectively. The Master on the IDE primary is called Primary Master, for example and a slave on the secondary IDE would be called the Secondary Slave. This configuration is necessary for BIOS to distinguish them for access and also determines the drive letters.

A hard disk configured as a Master will receive the letter C:, while another configured as a Slave will have the letter D:. Obviously the letters may change if the disk is divided into several partitions. Partitioning of the hard disk will be studied in depth in the next chapter

The configuration of Master or Slave is made through jumpers found on the hard disk or CD-ROM. The position of the jumpers for the desired status is found in the disk's manual. In case you don't have the manual, don't worry, you will almost always find a table of the options printed on the upper part of the hard disk.:

HARDWARE PC

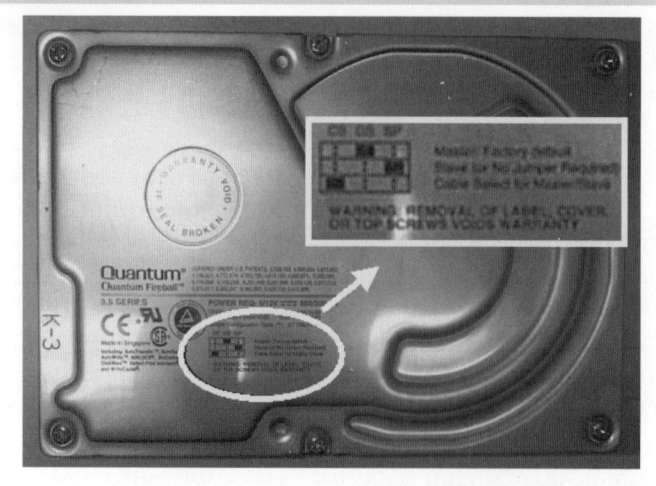

Generally there are only three options in the table: **Master**, **Slave** e **Cable Select**. The Cable Select option is a type of Plug and Play for hard disks and when this option is chosen, the disk connected at the end of the IDE cable will automatically be considered as a Master, while the other in the middle of the cable will be recognized as a slave.

The only problem with this is that for Cable Select to function you need a special ribbon cable and for this reason it is little used. When the disks are configured as Master and Slave, it does not matter which plug they are connected to on the IDE cable. The master may be connected to the middle plug, for example, without any problem, what matters are the jumper settings.

On a controller, one of the disks MUST be configured as a Master and if there is another, as a Slave. If they are both Masters, or both Slaves, there will be a conflict and neither will function.

In some disks as well as the options of Master, Slave and Cable Select, you will also find the options **One Drive Only** and **Drive is Master, Slave is Present**. In this case the option one drive only indicates that the drive will be installed as a Master and there is not a slave attached. The option Drive is Master, Slave is Present, indicates that the disk will be installed as a Master and that there will also be a Slave installed.

A last tip on this subject, if you remove the jumpers, with practically all hard disks, the HD will operate as a Slave. In case you cannot discover the jumper settings, use this tip to install the HD as a slave connected to another Master.

The position of the jumpers on the HD varies from model to model, but they are normally found between the sockets for the power and the ribbon cable, or if not, on the printed circuit underneath the HD.

Assembling and Configuring 121

In the case of IDE CD-ROMs, the jumper settings are even easier, being made with a single jumper with three positions situated at the rear of the drive wich allows it to be configured as a Master, Slave or Cable Select. This is usually marked above the pins showing the jumper options. MA signifies Master, SL Slave and CS Cable Select. It is almost universal standard that the middle position jumper is for a Slave, the right hand one is Master (viewed from behind) and the left hand one is Cable Select, exceptions to this are quite rare.

When two devices are connected to the same IDE interface both will share the interface, causing a loss of performance. For this reason it is always preferable when possible to install one on the Primary IDE and the other on the Secondary IDE. To install a HD and a CD-ROM for example, the best configuration would be with the HD as a Primary Master and the CD-ROM as a Secondary Master, or even Secondary Slave

FIXING THE DISK DRIVES

Well, we are almost there. Lets now install the diskette drive and the CD-ROM into their respective bays in the case. Diskette drives and HDs should be installed in the lower bays, whilst CD-ROMs and any other 5.25" drives (HDs or diskettes) should be placed in the upper bays.

To install the CD-ROM and the diskette drive, just remove the plastic cover plates and slide the unit in as shown in the following photos. To finish the installation screw the unit in place, using screws on both sides to keep it firmly in place.

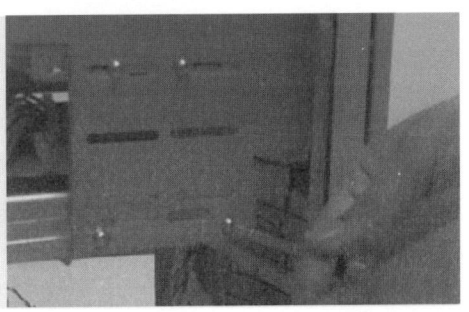

CONNECTING THE RIBBON AND POWER CABLES.

To complete the installation of the disk drives you only need to connect the ribbon and power cables. If you managed to survive the jumper configuration and the front panel wire connections then you will find this stage very simple. The only care to be taken is not to invert the ribbon cables or misplace the power connections.

To connect the ribbon cables properly, follow the red wire rule, where one side of the cable is marked in red, and is always connected to pin 1. To determine which is pin 1 of the IDE connector on the motherboard, consult the manual or look closely at the circuit around the connector, where you will see 1 marked. The same applies to the diskette drive

The red stripe on the cable should coincide with the number 1 marked on the motherboard. (shown circled).

When connecting the other end of the cable to the HD, CD-ROM or diskette drive the rule is the same, always place the side with a red stripe in pin 1 of the connector. Normally the red stripe is on the same side as the power cable but there are sometimes exceptions. The red rule always applies, this is standard.

Showing pin 1 marked on the circuit board of an HD.

Many times the connector on the motherboard has a plastic socket with a keyway that only permits its insertion one way round.

Assembling and Configuring **123**

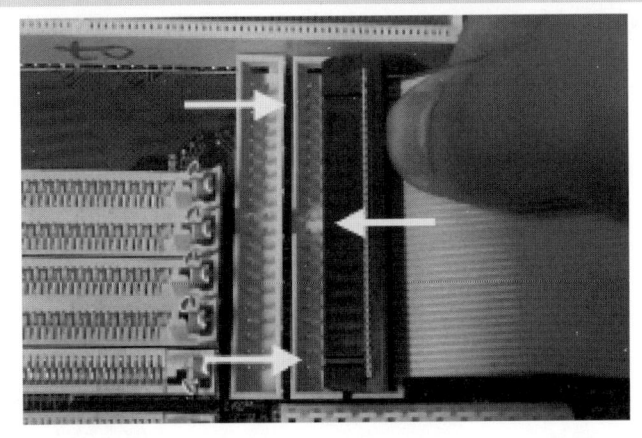

This keyway is often found in the sockets of most HDs and diskette drives, just ensure that the keyed side fits in the keyway.

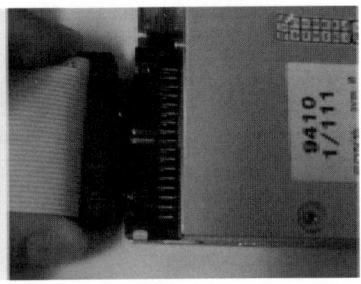

The connection of the power cable is also simple, with HDs and CD-ROMS, you don't need to worry, because it will only fit one way as the corners are chamfered, it is only possible to invert or misplace the cable with diskette drives. The correct diskette position is shown as follows.

Whilst finalizing the connection of the cables, take advantage of the occasion to connect the audio cable that goes from the CD-ROM to the sound card. Without this you will not be able to listen to audio CDS on the computer.

FINALIZING THE ASSEMBLY

We have purposely installed the processor, memory, front panel connectors, ribbon cables, disk drives etc, and configured all the jumpers, leaving the installation of the motherboard

HARDWARE PC

on it's base plate until last, in order to facilitate the installation. To continue the installation we should now fix the metal base plate with the motherboard mounted on it into place in the computer case, and connect the other components to it.

PLUGGING THE POWER CABLE

With AT power supplies you will find two power cables to be connected to the motherboard, pay attention to the color of the wires, and plug them in with both the black wires side by side in the middle. Be careful not to swap the position of the cables and leave the black wires on the outside, as this might damage the motherboard.

The power cable of an ATX is easier to plug in, you don't even need to worry about the positions of the black wires as the plug and socket are different and as well as having a chamfered corner, it has a little plastic latch that only permits it to be inserted one way round.

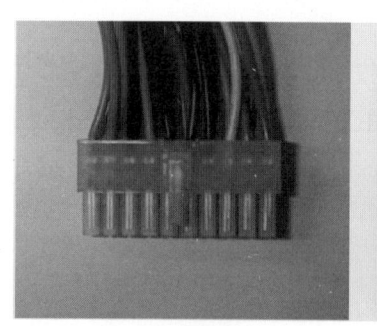

CONNECTING THE SERIAL AND PARALLEL CABLES

There are usually two serial and one parallel interfaces to be found on the motherboard, and in the majority of cases a PS/2 port as well. We use cables to connect these ports to the sockets at the back of the case, where we connect the mouse, printers etc and any other devices that use these ports.

The serial ports have 10 pins (two rows of 5) whilst the parallel port has 26 pins (two rows of 13). PS/2 ports have only 6 pins that are arranged in the form of a "C".

As with the other ribbons cables, pin 1 is always marked with a red stripe so as not to invert the cables. Again you need to resort to the manual or the indications of pin 1 on the motherboard to verify which is pin 1. Not that all the cables will have the red stripe to the same side, if you know the correct side of one, the others will be the same. Don't worry about the OS/2 port because two holes are blocked in the plug, it can only be fitted one way.

Usually there are serial cables with both 9 and 25 pins. The connector to the motherboard is the same with both, only the external socket is different. 25 pin sockets are an old standard, rarely used nowadays.

It does not matter whether you fix the sockets with their plates into the slots at the back of the case, or whether you remove them and fix them from these and screw them directly into the back of the computer case, where there are some cutouts reserved for them close to the power supply. The latter way is better, if only to permit more rational use of the space within the case. To fix them you can use the hexagonal nut drivers if you have one, or a pair of long nosed pliers.

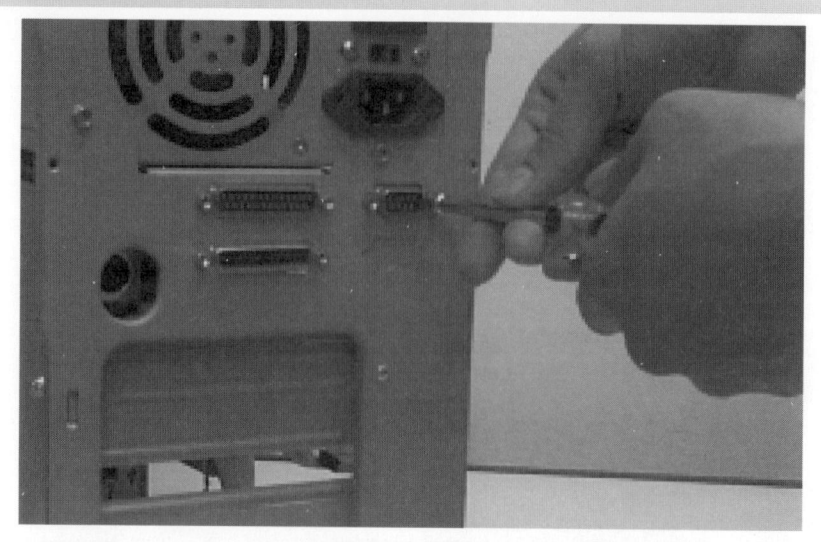

With ATX motherboards you will not have the work of installing any cables, because the serial, parallel, USB, OS/2 ports are all built in to the back part of the motherboard as shown below, and this fits directly into an opening in the cabinet.

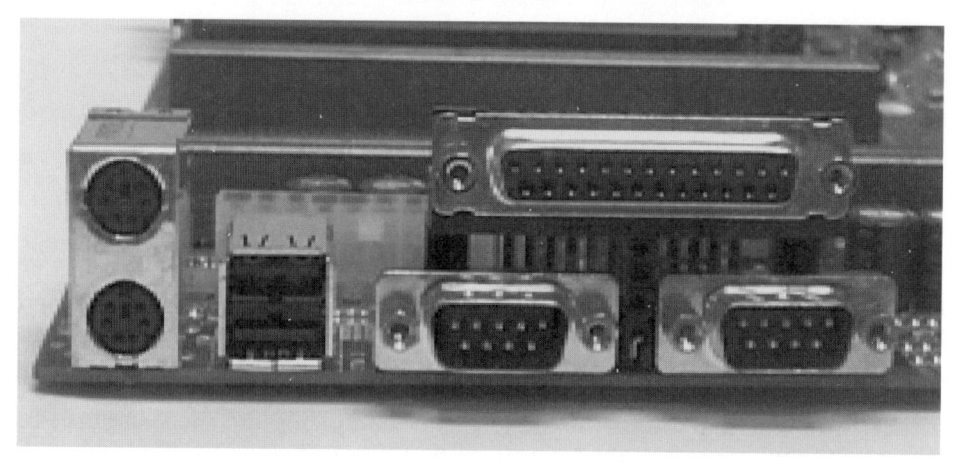

FITTING ISA, PCI AND AGP CARDS

Fitting video cards, sound cards, modems, SCSI cards and any other peripheral is pretty simple. It doesn't matter if it is PCI, ISA, AGP, VLB, etc., just press them into their slots like a video game cartridge and then fix them in place with a screw to the back of the case. It is not necessary to use much force, just place the card above the slot, and press down on one end, and then the other until it is firmly in place.

Motherboards with on board sound and video come with the appropriate ribbon cables that should be connected to the correct pin connectors on the motherboard. The only precaution, is, as always, to ensure that the red stripe is connected to pin 1.

FINISHING THE ASSEMBLY

Having finished assembling the computer, close the case, connect the keyboard, mouse, printer and other external peripherals. You will observe that the power supply in the case has two sockets. The bottom one, obviously should be connected to the mains, whilst the top one serves as an extension, which may be used to connect the monitor power. It makes no difference whether you connect the monitor directly to the power or to the power supply in the computer, because it is only connected as an extension of the other.

If you have correctly followed all the instructions and there are no damaged hardware components, then when the computer is switched on the first thing you will see is the computer counting its memory which indicates that it is apparently functioning (so far) without problems. However nothing may appear on the screen, or you may only hear intermittent beeps or maybe the computer doesn't show any signs of life at all in which case we have a problem. But as life is made of challenges, breathe deeply and get down to work. If everything functioned the first time, life would be pretty boring, wouldn't it?

PROBLEM SOLVING

Badly fitting or misplaced cables, defective RAM or cache memory, faulty video cards, defective motherboards, or incompatibility between some of the components are only some of the many reasons that cause a computer not to work.

The most common problem is when the computer is switched on there is no image on the screen and it just emits a series of beeps. These beeps are emitted by BIOS and give valuable indications as to what is wrong. In the beginning, if the computer is apparently inactive and you don't hear any beeps wait a while before switching off because sometimes BIOS takes one or two minutes to test the hardware before beginning to emit any error beeps. You will find a table with a complete list of all the beeps and their meanings in chapter 16.

First check that all the cables are properly plugged in, and the correct way round. Experiment and try removing them one at a time. If this doesn't work, remove all the expansion cards and disconnect all disk drives etc, leaving only the video card, processor, and the memory, because sometimes badly behaved cards can cause conflicts that impede the computer booting up. If the computer now starts normally, reconnect the peripherals one at a time to discover which is causing the problem.

It is also possible that the video card or memory is badly placed, or has a bad contact. Try removing them and cleaning the contacts with an eraser, before replacing them firmly in the proper places.

If the problem still persists, try changing the video card and memory to another position, because in rare cases some combinations cause mysterious conflicts with low quality motherboards. If it still doesn't work, then probably some component is damaged. In this case you will have to test each one separately to determine which one is causing the problem. The easiest way to do this is to beg, borrow or steal another computer which is functioning perfectly and substitute the pieces one at a time until you discover which one is defective. The biggest suspects are memory, followed by motherboards and video cards.

If the computer doesn't give any sign of life, not even a beep, but the power supply ventilator is turning, check that the ribbon cables to the disk drives are not inverted, this is very common and easy to do, even for experienced people. If this is the case, just replace them the right way round and switch on again. If the cables are connected correctly, but the problem persists, remove all the expansion cards again, as in the previous example to verify by a process of elimination, and check that the speaker cable is connected correctly and not broken. Try another speaker. If the speaker is correctly connected, and after all these tests, the problem is probably in the motherboard.

Finally, if the computer is still lifeless and not even the ventilator of the power supply or processor cooler is turning, the problem is in the power supply. Check that the voltage source is correct 110 or 220 volts (there is a switch behind on the case power supply). If the problem continues, the power supply or stabilizer (if used), may have problems. Try changing them.

If it still doesn't work, don't insist. After all this your brain may be tired and confused. Take a walk around the block and try again later or the next day When you are not so tired it will be easier to find out what is wrong.

If the micro initializes normally but locks up after a short time of use, there may be a problem with the RAM memory or cache. Try entering in the Setup and disabling the L2 cache, and also at the same time increase to the maximum, the memory wait state times (for more details, see chapter 17 about configuration in the Setup). If the problem goes away, try lowering the wait state times and reactivate the cache (one thing at a time) until the problem comes back, thus isolating the cause of the problem.

If the problems continue, check that the processor is not overheating. Try the finger test, using the computer until it locks up, then open the computer up, remove the cooler and touch the processor with your finger. If you can't keep it there for 10 seconds, then your processor is overheating and may be causing these lockups. At the end of chapter 18 you will find instructions on how to improve the cooling of the processor.

If the problem still persists try changing the memory modules, because everything indicates a defect in RAM memory.

130 HARDWARE PC

10 Configuring CMOS Setup and Formating the HD

After assembling the computer the next step is to configure it at the software level, before you can begin to install the operating system. This second stage consists in configuring some basic options in the CMOS Setup and formatting the hard disk.

The basic part of the CMOS Setup consists only in detecting the hard disks installed, configuring the diskette drive and boot sequence, and adjusting the date and time of the computer. To access Setup, you normally press a certain key during the counting of memory. It is most common to press the DEL key, but some BIOS use the F10 key or even combinations of keys like Crtl + Alt + S, this may be shown on the screen during the boot sequence.

Within Setup enter into the "Standard CMOS Setup" or simply "Standard Setup" and configure the diskette drive for 3.5" 1.44Mb, which is the default nowadays, unless you are using something different, such as 2.8MB. If you don't have a diskette drive installed, choose the "none" option. While you are in this screen, take advantage of it to adjust the date and time.

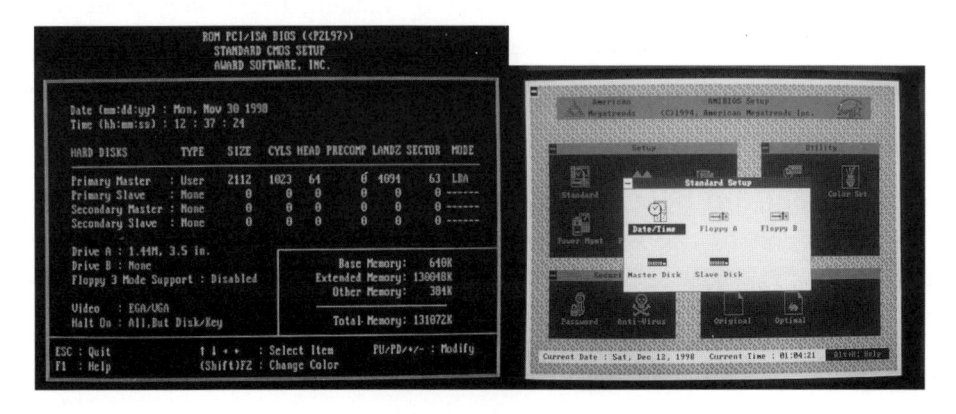

Standard CMOS Setup in an Award BIOS that uses a text interface (left) and an AMI BIOS that uses a graphical interface (right)

132 HARDWARE PC

Returning to the main menu of the Setup, now choose the "IDE HDD auto Detection" or "Auto IDE" option so that your hard disk(s) will be automatically detected. It may detect them all, end of story, or it may ask you to confirm each one, showing 1, 2 or 3 options permitting the HD to operate in **Normal**, **Large** or **LBA** mode. Nowadays with today's larger HDs choose the suggested option (LBA) and type Y or the corresponding number, usually 2 for LBA (In the photo at left for example, the correct number is 2).

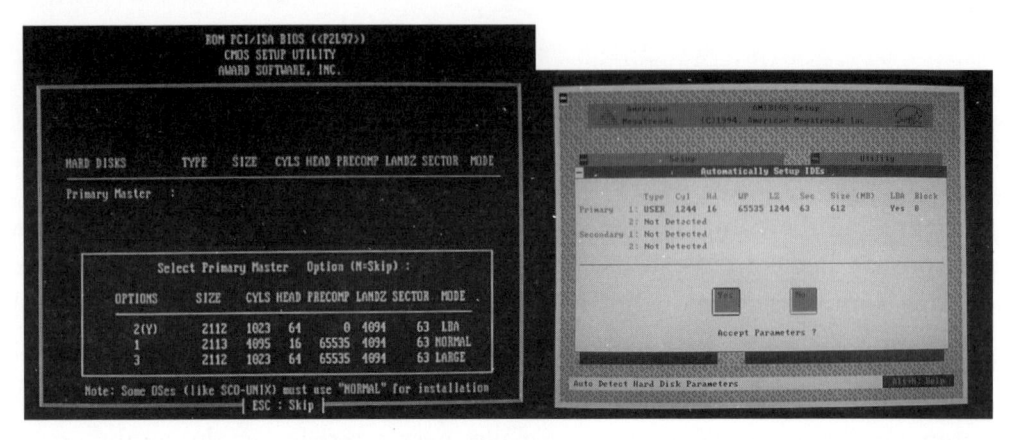

Automatic detection of IDE hard disks installed in an Award (left) BIOS and AMI (right)

To finish the configuration, just use the option Save & Exit found in the main menu which saves the configuration and exits. When using an AMI BIOS, just press the ESC key until a screen appears asking if you want to save the alterations.

OTHER CONFIGURATIONS

Although the configurations of the Setup that we have seen above are sufficient for the computer to function, it is worthwhile to look at some other options. As the majority of options assume the correct values by default, I will only quote those that should be looked at. The title refers to the relevant screen and the options are highlighted in bold text.

Advanced CMOS Setup

1st Boot, 2nd Boot, 3rd Boot and 4th Boot: This is generally found in AMI BIOSes and gives the option of choosing in which sequence the system will search for the operating system. You just select the sequence you want, choosing between floppies, HDs, CD-ROM etc.

Security Option (Password Check): You should have seen an option on the main Setup screen and option to use a password. Here we can choose between the option "Setup" and "Always" that sometimes is shown as system "System". If you choose the Setup option, you will be asked for a password every time you want to enter in the Setup. If you choose the option Always then you will be asked for a password every time that you switch on the computer. The use of the Setup password is quite useful because it restricts the use of the computer to only to people who know the password or just restricts the use of the Setup, to avoid the user changing things here.

PCI clock: Speed at which the PCI bus will operate. Choose 1/ 2 if the motherboard is functioning at 66 MHz or 1/3 if the motherboard is functioning at 100 MHz.

AGP CLK/CPU CLK: Bus frequency at which the AGP bus will operate. Choose 1/1 if the motherboard is functioning at 66 MHz and 2/3 if it is functioning at 100 MHz.

AGP Aperture Size: You should remember that the AGP bus permits a video card to use RAM memory to store textures. This option permits us to set the maximum amount of memory that the video card should use. It is recommendable to set this value to half the available RAM (32 MB if there is 64Mb for example)

Assign IRQ for VGA Card or Allocate IRQ to PCI VGA: This option permits you to reserve an IRQ for use by the video card. The majority of 3D video accelerator cards only function properly if this is enabled. Set to **enabled as** necessary.

Power Management

Power Management: Power Management which is a resource that permits the computer to save energy when it is not being used, may be enabled or disabled here. Usually you will find the following options:

Disabled: All energy saving features are disabled.

Min Saving: Power Management is enabled, but only enters into action after 45 or 60 minutes (depending on the BIOS) of inactivity, providing little saving.

Max Saving: Maximum saving, some components begin to be shut down after only a few minutes of inactivity.

User Defined: This option is the most indicated. You may set the options according to your use of the computer.

Integrated Peripherals

On Board Serial Port 1 e On Board Serial Port 2: This option permits disabling or changing the address for the serial ports of the computer. There are two serial ports, serial port 1 is normally used by the mouse, whilst the second may be used to connect two computers with a serial cable, an external modem, or any other device that requires a serial port.

By default the on board Serial Port 1, that is generally used by the mouse, uses COM

2 with an address of 3F8, in case you install a peripheral that is going to use this port (a modem configured for COM 1 for example) you may change the port used by the mouse to avoid conflicts. In other cases you may disable the second serial port to free up the address used by it.

Serial Port 1 IRQ e Serial Port 2 IRQ: here you can choose which IRQ will be used by the serial interfaces. The most common is to set Serial Port 1 to use IRQ 4 and Serial Port 2 to use IRQ 3 but in some cases you may need to choose other IRQs to solve conflicts.

On Board Parallel Port: This is nothing more than the parallel port that is used by the printer. Obviously we would normally never do this., because our printer and any other devices attached to the parallel port would not work. However in computers that don't have a printer, you can free up an IRQ by disabling this.

Parallel Port Address: Here you can choose which I/O (input/output) address will be used by the parallel port. There are three available addresses: 378, 278 and 3BC. If you only have one parallel port installed you may freely choose any one of these addresses. If there is a second parallel port installed in an ISA or PCI slot then each should have its own address. There may be up to 3 parallel ports installed in a computer.

You may acquire new parallel ports in the form of ISA, VLB or PCI cards that can be found with a little effort in computer shops. Another option is to buy a Super IDE card and disable all the options on it except for the printer.

Parallel Port IRQ: Like all devices, the parallel port also uses an IRQ. Usually this is set to IRQ 5 or 7, the last is the most recommended, seeing that IRQ is generally used by sound cards. Some BIOSes also permit the use of other IRQs.

On Board Parallel Port Mode (On Board Printer Mode): Parallel ports found in modern motherboards may operate in several different modes. Here we can select which mode to use. The options normally available are Normal, Bi-directional, ECP and EPP.

The Normal and Bi-directional modes are much slower. The difference between them is that Bi-directional mode permits bi-directional communications. The ECP mode is faster being used by newer printers, as well as being compatible with the majority of scanners, Zip drives and other devices that use the parallel port. There is also EPP that has a speed similar to ECP but with less resources.

Generally the parallel port is set to ECP because it has several advantages over the others, such as the use of a DMA channel that reduces the demands on the processor during data transfers. There may be, however, an older printer or other device that only functions with a bi-directional port. In that case just come back here and change the operating mode as desired.

ECP Mode use DMA: ECP ports use a DMA channel to reduce the load on the processor while the port is being used. A computer has a total of 8 DMA channels, the first 4 (numbered from 0 to 3) are 8 bits, while the other 4 are 16 bit channels. ECP channels always use 8 bits. As channel 2 is being used by the diskette drive interface, and channel 1 is usually used by the sound card, we can use channels 0 or 3.

Security

Password: This is the option that permits you to enter a password for the computer. It is necessary to type it twice to guard against any possibility of error.

In case you want to change the password BIOS will ask you to enter the old password first. The password I checked according to the options chosen in Security Option (Password Check) of the Advanced CMOS Setup, and may be required every time you switch on the computer or only when you want to make alterations in the setup.

Partitioning and formatting the hard disk

After setting the essential options in the Setup, the computer should be capable of initializing normally using a boot diskette. Quite a common problem at this point is that the busy light of the drive mysteriously stays lit indefinitely and the drive doesn't function. This happens when the ribbon cable to the drive is inverted. If this is the case, open the case and connect the cable the right way round, and the drive should function.

As the hard disk still doesn't have an operating system we need a boot disk to initialize the computer. Even if you are going to install Windows 95 it is recommendable to use a Windows 98 boot disk because this includes support for IDE and SCSI CD-ROM drives without having to alter the initialization files, which saves you having a headache when you have to install Windows from a CD-ROM. Ask a friend who has Windows 98 to make a boot disk for you.

After the boot, if you try to access drive C you will receive an error message, as if there was no hard disk installed in the computer, because it still needs to be formatted before it can be recognized by the operating system.

We studied two types of formatting in the chapter on hard disks, called physical format and logical format. Although the hard disk comes physically formatted from the factory, which permits BIOS to recognize it, we still need to do the logical format. There are several programs that can do this, but we will use the FDISK that is part of the Windows boot disk. Just type **A:\FDISK** to run it.

136 HARDWARE PC

Both Windows 95 OSR/2 (or Windows "B") and Windows 98 offer FAT 32 support. Only the older Windows did not support this filing system. When you use the FDISK from a Windows 98 or Windows 95 OSR/2 disk you will be asked in the beginning if you want support for large capacity disks. If you reply Yes, your disk will be formatted with a FAT 32, otherwise it will use the FAT 16.

```
Your computer has a disk larger than 512 MB. This version of Windows
includes improved support for large disks, resulting in more efficient
use of disk space on large drives, and allowing disks over 2 GB to be
formatted as a single drive.

IMPORTANT: If you enable large disk support and create any new drives on this
disk, you will not be able to access the new drive(s) using other operating
systems, including some versions of Windows 95 and Windows NT, as well as
earlier versions of Windows and MS-DOS. In addition, disk utilites that
were not designed explicitly for the FAT32 file system will not be able
to work with this disk. If you need to access this disk with other operating
systems or older disk utilities, do not enable large drive support.

Do you wish to enable large disk support (Y/N)...........? [N]
```

As we saw in the chapter on hard disks, each cluster in a FAT 16 may not be larger than 32 Kbytes, and each FAT 16 partition may not be greater than 2 Gigabytes. Another problem in ☐ using clusters of 32 Kbytes is that there is a great waste of disk space, because each cluster cannot contain more than one file.

Due to its limitations Fat 16 is completely inadequate for modern disks. To partition an 8GB disk you would have to make 4 partitions using a FAT 16. Fat 32 overcomes these limitations, permitting partitions of up to 2 terabytes (1 terabyte = 1.024 Gigabytes) with clusters of only 4K bytes in partitions less than 8 GB.

Fat 32 is not compatible with the first version of Windows 95 only with the OSR/2 version or Windows 98. If you try to install an older Windows version to a disk formatted with FAT 32, you will receive an error message because the system will not be able to access the disk.

After choosing to use a large filing system or not, the main menu of Fdisk appears, where there are 5:

1. Create a partition or logical DOS unit: permits the creation of partitions on the disk.

2. Set Active Partition: permits defining which partition will be used for booting the system. There must be one, and only one, active partition defined, or else it will not be possible to boot from the HD.

3. Delete partition or logical DOS unit: permits previously created partitions to be excluded. When a partition is deleted all information in it is lost.

4. Display partition information: shows information about the partitions.

5. Alter the drive unit: This option is only shown if you have 2 HDs or more, permits you to choose which hard disk to configure.

If you choose the first option, a new menu with 3 options appears "Create a primary DOS partition" "Create an extended DOS partition" and "Create logical units in an extended DOS partition". To return to a previous menu press ESC.

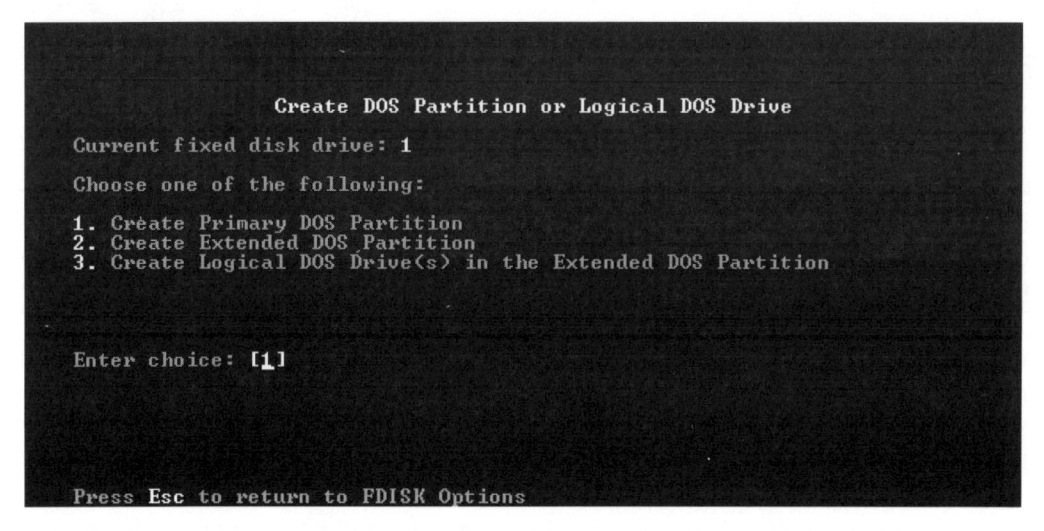

```
                Create DOS Partition or Logical DOS Drive
Current fixed disk drive: 1

Choose one of the following:

  1. Create Primary DOS Partition
  2. Create Extended DOS Partition
  3. Create Logical DOS Drive(s) in the Extended DOS Partition



Enter choice: [1]




Press Esc to return to FDISK Options
```

The **primary partition** will be the letter C:\ of your hard disk and will be used to initialize the computer. Fdisk permits the creation of only one primary partition. To partition the disk in two or more partitions an **extended partition** should also be created that which include all the other partitions of the disk.

Dividing the hard disk into several partitions has several advantages, such as the possibility of installing different operating systems in the same disks, and organizing stored files better. From the point of view of the operating system each partition is a separate hard disk and appears with its own drive letter.

The use of more than one partition also brings a little more security. Using two partitions (C and D), one for the operating system, and one for the files for example, you can even format the C partition and your files remain intact on drive D. This division also brings a greater protection against viruses because many only attack the C drive, your files will be better protected in a separate drive.

FORMATTING THE HD WITH ONLY ONE PARTITION

To create a primary partition on the disk, choose the option, **"create a primary DOS partition"** from the previous menu. Fdisk will make a quick test of the hard disk and then ask if you want to make the primary partition occupy all available space and to make this the active partition. If you want to partition the disk as one unit, reply "Yes". Fdisk will make a quick check again and the disk will be partitioned with a single partition. In this case, our work with Fdisk is complete and you just need to press ESC twice to exit the program. Another message appears saying that the changes will not come into effect until you reinitialize the system. Press Esc again to quit, and reinitialize the computer in order to format the HD.

After reinitializing the computer, if you try to access drive C there will be an error message saying "Invalid media type reading drive C" "Abort, Retry, Fail?". This happens because Fdisk doesn't format the hard disk, its function is only to establish the partitions and the filing system that will be used for each partition. Now we need our tried and trusty friend FORMAT to actually format the hard disk before it can be used. The syntax of the format command is FORMAT followed by a space and the drive letter to be formatted. To format drive C for example, use the command **"FORMAT C:"**

You will be asked if you really want to format the drive, and if you reply Yes, the formatting will begin. The bigger the disk, the longer the format will take.

DIVIDING THE HD INTO SEVERAL PARTITIONS

To divide the hard disk into two or more partitions the primary partition should first be created using only a part of the hard disk. To do this, reply No when Fdisk asks if you want to use all the available space for a DOS partition.

You should then tell it the size of the partition that you want to create. This may be a number of Megabytes, or a percentage. In the photo on the left, a primary partition occupying half the disk was created. A new screen showing that a partition was created and that 50% of the space on the disk is available for new partitions.

After creating the primary partition we should create an extended partition using the rest of the disk space, because Fdisk only permits the use of a single primary partition. This partition will encompass all the other disk partitions of the disk. Return to the main menu of Fdisk and choose the "Create partition or a logical DOS unit" option again and in following the option "Create an Extended DOS partition".

You will be asked for the desired partition size. Simply press Enter in order to create a partition using all the available space on the disk. Again an information screen will be shown, showing that the disk has, in addition to the primary partition, and an extended partition, and that all the space is used.

After creating the extended partition it should be divided into logical units. After pressing ESC, Fdisk will exhibit a message showing that no logical units are defined and will ask for the size of the logical partition that is to be created in the extended partition. You may enter a value in Megabytes, or as a percentage.

So that the logical unit occupies all the space in the extended partition, you just have to press Enter. If you want more than two partitions on the disk, just create a logical unit occupying only a part of the space in the extended unit. In this case, after creating the partition, Fdisk will inform you that there is still free space and give the option to create another logical unit. You may create new units until the space available runs out.

DEFINING AN ACTIVE PARTITION

When you return to the main menu of Fdisk, you will see a message saying that there is no active partition and it is necessary to activate the primary partition in order that the disk be bootable.

From the main menu choose the option "Define active partition" and in the following screen where you asked which partition should be activated, choose your primary partition. Now, you just have to exit from Fdisk and format the disk. Note that each partition has a separate drive letter because from the point of view of the operating system they are separate disks. Each partition must be formatted separately.

In the other example, the primary partition was automatically defined as active when we chose to make this occupy the whole disk. When you create several partitions the process is no longer automatic.

EXCLUDING PARTITIONS

 To exclude partitions we use the third option of Fdisk. A new screen comes up showing options to exclude the primary partition of the disk, exclude an extended partition, exclude a logical partition within an extended partition, or exclude a NON-DOS partition (a partition not supported by Windows 95/98, such as NTFS, HPF3, or LINUX).

```
                Delete DOS Partition or Logical DOS Drive
Current fixed disk drive: 1

Choose one of the following:

  1. Delete Primary DOS Partition
  2. Delete Extended DOS Partition
  3. Delete Logical DOS Drive(s) in the Extended DOS Partition
  4. Delete Non-DOS Partition


Enter choice: [ ]




Press Esc to return to FDISK Options
```

Generally the option to exclude partitions is used when you want to return to a disk with a single partition after having divided it into several, but you may use this to convert units with a FAT 16 to a FAT 32, for example.

There is no mystery to these options. Just choose the partition to be excluded and confirm the volume name (that is an arbitrary name you gave it when you formatted it) and appears above in the column "Volume". In case the volume has no name, just press Enter. Fdisk will ask if you are sure you want to delete the partition, and if you are, then just reply Yes.

To exclude an extended partition we must first delete all the logical units within it, using the option "Exclude logical units of an extended DOS partition", and only after this can you delete the extended partition. It is worth remembering once again , when a partition is excluded all the data stored in it is lost.

If you have a hard disk at hand formatted with a non-DOS system (not supported by Windows 95/98) such as NTFS (used by Windows NT), HPFS (used by OS/2), or a Linux system and you want to format it with a FAT 16 or a FAT 32 for use in conjunction with your version of Windows, just use the option "Exclude a non-DOS partition" to eliminate its format, and then re-create a partition with a FAT system.

INSTALLING A SECOND HARD DISK

When installing a second hard disk as a primary slave, you just have to repeat the previous procedures to format it because the disk will only be recognized by the operating system after it has been duly partitioned and formatted.

When Fdisk starts, by default, it will show you primary master disk. To access the second disk that you want to partition, choose option number 5 (Alter the current fixed disk) on the main menu. A list of all the installed hard disks will be shown as well as their logical partitions. Enter the number that corresponds to your new hard disk and partition it as you wish as previously described.

Note that when you install a second hard disk all the drive letters will be altered. Lets say that you had a disk divided into two partitions called "Windows" and "Files" that appeared as **C:** and **D:** respectively. When a new disk formatted with a single primary partition called "New" is installed, the partition "Files" that previously appeared as **D:**, now becomes **E:**, and the partiton "New" of the hard disk will receive the letter **D:**. The CD-ROM receives the next available letter after the hard disks:

*B*EFORE

C: "Windows"
D: "Files"
E:"CD-ROM"

*A*FTER

C: "Windows"
D:"New"
E:"Files"
F:"CD-ROM"

The rule is that the primary partition of the principal disk always will be the letter C and the primary partition of a second disk will always be D. The other logical partitions of both disks will receive letters in sequence after this.

11 INSTALLING WINDOWS AND CONFIGURING THE HARDWARE

After partitioning and formatting the hard disk, we only have to install the operating system to make the computer ready for use.

INSTALLING WINDOWS

Although there is no problem in installing Windows directly from the CD-ROM, it is more practical to copy the installation files to the hard disk and install it from there, because as well as reducing the installation time you will always have a copy of these files on your hard disk wich saves you the trouble of looking for the CD every time you want to install a new peripheral or update drivers etc, as it always asks you to place the CD-ROM in the drive, as well as facilitating any future re-installations.

To copy the installation files, create a folder in your hard disk called "Winsetup", for example, and copy all the files in the root directory of your Windows 95 CD, or those which are in the directory WIN98 of the Windows 98 CD. The files occupy about 50Mb for Windows 95 and about 100Mb for Windows 98. You just need to copy the CAB files and the executables etc, there is no need to copy sub folders/directories. Use the command **"copy *.* c:\winsetup"** from within the folder on the CD where the files are located and this will copy all you need.

Copying the installation files from your CD to the hard disk is not considered piracy (unless your CD is a pirate copy) because you are legally allowed to make a backup copy of the software.

To the contrary of other operating systems, Windows installation is extremely simple and intuitive. The installation processes of both Windows 95 and Windows 98 are similar, all that changes is the graphic interface. I will only give one explanation which serves for both, just quoting any differences exist.

To run the installation program, just go to the directory/folder where you copied the installation files of Windows (or the CD-ROM) and type "INSTALL"

Scandisk will automatically be executed to verify if there are any logical errors in the hard disk. The installation can only continue after any errors have been corrected.

After Scandisk has been executed, the Windows installation program finally enters into action. Soon after the installation wizard has loaded, the license contract will be shown to you asking if you accept the terms and conditions. Obviously Windows will only be installed if you accept them, so reply Yes, or else go and look for a different operating system.

The next step is to choose the folder where Windows will be installed. The folder Windows" will be suggested, but you may change this to any other you want. A new screen then appears with a list of options and accessories which permit you to choose what you want to install. The most recommended is the personalized installation which permits you to choose which components to install one by one.

After continuing, a dialog Box appears where you should fill in your name (or any other) and company name if wanted. Following this you will have to fill in the serial number as well. This should be on a label on the plastic CD jewel box.

In Windows 95 the next stage is the configuration of the network. In the identification window you should give a name to your computer, the name of the workgroup and a description of the computer. This data will identify the computer to the network. In case the computer is not going to be connected to a network, just fill in the blanks with fictitious names. You will then be asked which protocols you want to install. To access Internet you will need only a dial-up adapter (modem) and a TCP/IP protocol. To use the connection via Windows cable you should also install the client for Microsoft networks and the NetBeui protocol. In case the computer is to be connected to a network you should also install the network protocols (generally IPX/SPX or NetBeui). These can be changed later using the Network icon in the Control Panel.

After configuring the network ambience you will be shown a list of hardware components which were detected during the installation. You may freely change the list now, or leave it until later and make any changes using the Control Panel when the installation has finished.

Windows will then ask if you want to create an emergency disk (boot disk) and ask for a blank diskette to be placed in drive A. It does not matter whether you create one now or not because you may create as many as you want whenever you want through the add/remove programs, boot disk option in the Control Panel. If you want to create a boot disk later, you will be asked for the Windows installation disks.

Finally the files will start being copied. Take advantage of this to go and have a cup of coffee because it will take 5 or 10 minutes, and after it finishes there will not be much else to do.

When the file copies have finished the system will be reinitialized and the installation continues with the detection and installation of the plug and play devices and other configurations. Again this process is automatic and takes a while, go and have another coffee!

To finish the installation you will be shown a window where you should choose the time zone where you live, and may also correct the date and time. If you are installing Windows 95, this will soon be followed soon by the printer installation wizard. You can install a printer now, or simply cancel it and leave it for later.

The system will be re-initialized one more time and the installation will be concluded.

CONFIGURING THE HARDWARE

The installation of hardware in Windows 95/98 is always made using a device "driver". A device driver is a small program file that functions like an instruction manual giving Windows all the information it needs about the respective sound card, video card etc and teaching Windows how it functions and what to do with it.

Windows has a large library of drivers supplied by the manufacturers that permits the automatic installation of various peripherals like sound cards from SoundBlaster, the majority of video cards, and most modems, printers, IDE CD-ROMs, SCSI cards, as well as the basic inbuilt hardware of the computer, such as IDE interfaces, serial and parallel ports, diskette drives, and in the case of Windows 98, USB ports, UDMA drivers etc. In spite of being very large, it does not have everything because there are always new models coming out, and it becomes out of date.

In case Windows doesn't have a driver for the device it will ask for a disk supplied by the manufacturer. You should then insert the diskette or CD-ROM that contains the files and indicate where they are to be found.

In other cases a generic driver may be installed, which, while it does the job, doesn't permit Windows to take full advantage of the device's resources. This should, if possible, then be updated with the manufacturer supplied drivers. For example, if you have a Trident 9680 video card in Windows 95, Windows will use the standard "Trident Super VGA" driver that only permits the use of 256 colors. If you install the drivers that come with the card, Windows will then be able to show 16 millions colors.

Even time you buy any hardware component, video card, sound card, modem, motherboard, printer, scanner, zip drive etc, insist on the CD or diskette which has the drivers, without this it will be impossible to install it properly and make it function.

The use of drivers by Window guarantees a superior performance of the device because all of its facilities may be used, as the drivers are written by the manufacturers themselves, and nobody knows the hardware better than they do. Generally newer device drivers increase the compatibility and correct any known bugs in older versions, as well as increasing the performance of the device through better and more rational use of its resources.

You can see all the devices which are installed and the addresses, IRQs etc they are using by accessing the Control Panel, System, device "manager".

FINDING FILES

You have got the manufacturers CD in your hands but can't manage to find the drivers for you card on it? Don't worry, this always happens, because usually the manufacturers include drivers for several different devices on the same CD, not just for that which you bought. As well as this, they include drivers for other operating systems, Windows 3.1, Windows 95, Windows 98, Windows NT + 2000 etc, and also in addition you will find manuals and other programs that turn the CD into a jungle of files.

To help you understand this hierarchy of device driver files etc, we are going to take 3 common CDs as examples, one for a Trident video card, one for a Crystal sound card, and one for a PC100 motherboard (which has sound, video, modem and network on-board).

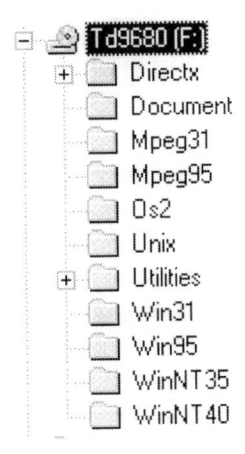

Installing Windows And Configuring the Hardware 147

```
─ Td9680 (F:)
  ├─ Directx
  ├─ Document
  ├─ Mpeg31
  ├─ Mpeg95
  ├─ Os2
  ├─ Unix
  ├─ Utilities
  ├─ Win31
  ├─ Win95
  ├─ WinNT35
  └─ WinNT40
```

In the CD for the Trident video card there are drivers for Windows 3.1 (in the folder Win31), for Windows 95 (folder Win95) and for Windows NT (in the folders WinNT35 and WinNT40) as well as drivers for OS/2 and Unix. To install this card in Windows 98, use the Windows 95 drivers. The other folders contain DirectX installation files and some utilities. The folder Document contains the manual for the video card.

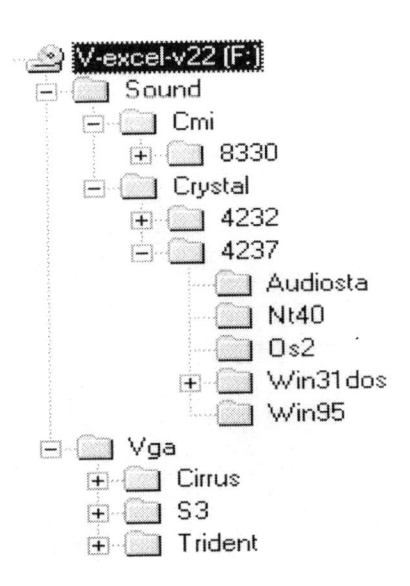

```
V-excel-v22 (F:)
├─ Sound
│  ├─ Cmi
│  │  └─ 8330
│  └─ Crystal
│     ├─ 4232
│     └─ 4237
│        ├─ Audiosta
│        ├─ Nt40
│        ├─ Os2
│        ├─ Win31dos
│        └─ Win95
└─ Vga
   ├─ Cirrus
   ├─ S3
   └─ Trident
```

In the CD for the Cristal sound card (model 4237,) we have an even richer example. First there are two folders with drivers for the sound card (folder Sound) and an-

148 HARDWARE PC

other with video card drivers (folder VGA). Opening the folder for sound drivers there is now a division for CMI sound cards and Cristal sound cards. Opening the folder for the Cristal drivers you will find drivers for the 4232 and 4237 cards. As the card is a 4237 we open the folder with drivers for it and finally we find sub folders with drivers for Windows 95, Windows NT 4, Windows 3.1 and OS/2.

There is also a program to play audio CDs and WAV files in the folder called Audiosta.

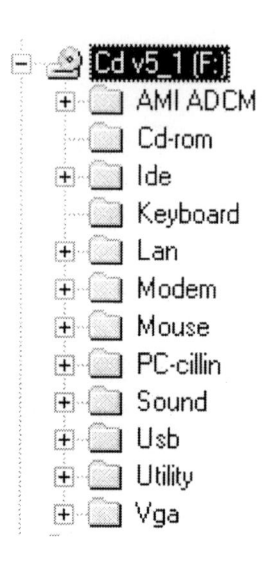

```
- Cd v5_1 (F:)
  + AMI ADCM
    Cd-rom
  + Ide
    Keyboard
  + Lan
  + Modem
  + Mouse
  + PC-cillin
  + Sound
  + Usb
  + Utility
  + Vga
```

To finish our examples we have a CD that comes with a PC100 motherboard. The CD has drivers for all the on-board components, video (folder VGA), sound (folder sound), modem (folder modem), and network (folder LAN). Within each folder there are drivers for various operating systems. There are also drivers to activate the USB in Windows 95 (folder USB).

OBTAINING UPDATED DRIVERS

All good peripheral manufacturers keep their drivers under constant development. This constant improvement guarantees that drivers are always better, both in terms of compatibility and in performance. You can download the latest drivers free from the manufacturers site on Internet.

A good site to find drivers on Internet is WinFiles which has practically all the available drivers for Windows 95, 98, NT and CE divided by category, such as video cards, modems, sound cards etc, and then by manufacturers. To find the newest driver for a Trident 9750 video card for example, just click on "Video Adapters" and then "Trident". The URL of Winfiles is: **http://winfiles.com/drivers**.

As well as Winfiles there are other sites that have updated drivers available. Good places to look are:

http://www.windrivers.com

http://www.drivershq.com

http://www.driverguide.com/

http://www.driverforum.com/

http://www.driverzone.com/

The possibility of getting drivers using Internet is extremely useful when you need to install some device but don't have the drivers for it. You just need to know the make and model to find the right drivers for it.

INSTALLING VIDEO CARDS

Both Windows 95 and 98 are capable of detecting any video card installed in the computer. The problem is that often a generic driver is installed that whilst it functions, doesn't take advantage of all the card's resources. This problem is more notable in Windows 95 whose library is well out of date nowadays.

At other times Windows simply doesn't have any suitable driver for the card and installs the generic "Standard VGA" that functions with any VGA, SVGA or 3D card, but limits the video card to 16 colors and a resolution of 640x480. In this case changing the driver is a priority. In other cases Windows will have suitable drivers and their replacement is not necessary.

To alter video card drivers you should access the video properties through the video icon in the Control Panel, or simply by right clicking on a blank part of the screen and then choosing "Properties". Now click on "Configurations" and then the "Advanced Properties" button.

A description of the installed files, their version number and the files used. In the photo a generic "Trident Super VGA" driver is being used that only permits the use of 256 colors. To update the driver, just click on the "Alter" button.

A menu will then be shown with the video card drivers Windows has. Click on the "Have disk" button, and tell Windows where to find the manufacturer supplier drivers by using the Search, click to confirm and the driver installation will be started.

In case you are using Windows 98, the driver update wizard will appear asking if you want it to search for an updated driver, or simply show a list of available drivers in a certain area. As we are going to install the manufacturer supplied drivers, choose the

150 HARDWARE PC

second option and indicate the location of the drivers.

You may receive messages about version conflicts. These messages arise when the installation program is trying to substitute one of your system's files by an older version. Windows intercepts this attempt and asks if you want to keep the current file or replace it.

Usually you would reply Yes to keep the current file because the older version would have less resources than the current one, and may cause problems.

However it sometimes happens that even being older, the manufacturer supplier driver is better than the generic Windows driver. This seems strange, Doesn`t it? Not really, for example many current video cards use Trident chipsets. Trident however only manufactures and sells chipsets, the video cards are assembled by hundreds of other manufacturers and are usually sold only with reference to the chipset used such as: "Trident 9680", "Trident Provideo 9685", "Trident 9750" etc.

Each manufacturer then develops the drivers most suitable for their own boards that obviously will always be a little different from the generic drivers supplied by Trident and included in Windows' library. In this case, even being older, the manufacturer supplied drivers are probably better than the generic drivers supplied by Trident.

One recommendation is that you note the names of the files used by the old driver shown in the "Advanced display properties" Window and allow the replacement of these files only. This will guarantee that the driver will effectively be installed without replacing any of the Windows system files.

Many cards, especially the latest 3D ones have a driver installation assistant in their installation CD-ROM. Just have a look within the drivers folder to see if there is a file called "Setup", "Config" or "Install'. In this case, instead of using the previous method, you just need to execute the program on the CD-ROM and all the drivers will be installed automatically. In case there are any messages of conflicts, use the same techniques as described previously.

INSTALLING THE MONITOR

Although this is not a great priority, it is useful to install or configure the monitor that we are using otherwise Windows will not know the resolutions and refresh rates supported by the monitor. As a result of this, if you try to use a higher resolution or refresh rate than that supported, the monitor will lose its synchronization and you will just see a lots of lines etc., like a TV out of tune. In this case you will have to re-enter Windows in safe mode (because this mode uses a resolution of 640x480, 16 colors and a 60 Hz refresh rate, a configuration supported by any VGA or SVGA monitor) to re-configure the video settings. When the monitor is correctly configured this can never happen because Windows would not permit the use of a non-supported video mode.

To adjust the monitor settings, access the video properties again in the "Configuration" screen, enter in "Advanced properties" and access the "Monitor" section. Click the "Alter" button and mark the "show all devices" option. Now choose the make and then the model of your monitor. All the manufacturers are listed on the left side and their respective available models are shown on the right side. In case you have a diskette or CD supplied by the manufacturer you may use this by clicking on the " Have disk" option. In case your monitor is not shown on the list, try a "plug and play" monitor.

INSTALLING SOUND CARDS

The installation of plug and play sound cards is fairly simple, in Windows 98 and even in Windows 95 it is not difficult. After the card is physically installed, just initialize Windows and the new hardware should be detected automatically. Depending on the sound

152 HARDWARE PC

card model, if Windows already has suitable drivers it will install it automatically, requiring only, maybe, that you tell it where the installation files of Windows are (In case you installed Windows from your HD and the files are still there, it will use them automatically without any messages at all, otherwise it will ask for a Windows CD). In other cases it will ask for the manufacturer supplied disk, and you should just tell it where to find it.

A message will be shown in Windows 95 asking where to find the sound card drivers. Click on the button "Search" and a new window will be opened. In the drop down list below click on the drive that contains the disk with the drivers (e.g. CD-ROM or diskette) and from the menu above select the folder where the drivers are. When you have finished, click OK to close the open windows, and again OK in the next window. You may also be asked for the installation files of Windows, be proceed as before.

In Windows 98 the menu is different but the procedure is almost the same. Choose "Search for the best device driver" and then "Specify an area". Now click on the "Search" button and indicate the folder where the drivers are. When you have finished, click on the "Advance" button.

If you need to install a sound card but don't have its drivers, don't despair. Even if you haven't got the proper drivers, Windows will be able to tell you what make and model it is when it detects the new hardware. Then it becomes easy to find the drivers on Internet, p.e. WinFiles.

Maybe you will find difficulties in installing some on-board sound cards, because with many of these the installation procedure is a little different. You need to execute a program to install the sound card, usually called **"unidrv.exe"** which can be found in the sound drivers folder in the CD which comes with the motherboard. After running this program the computer will be re-initialized and a new windows "new hardware found" will be shown, and then you just indicate the folder/directory where the sound drivers are.

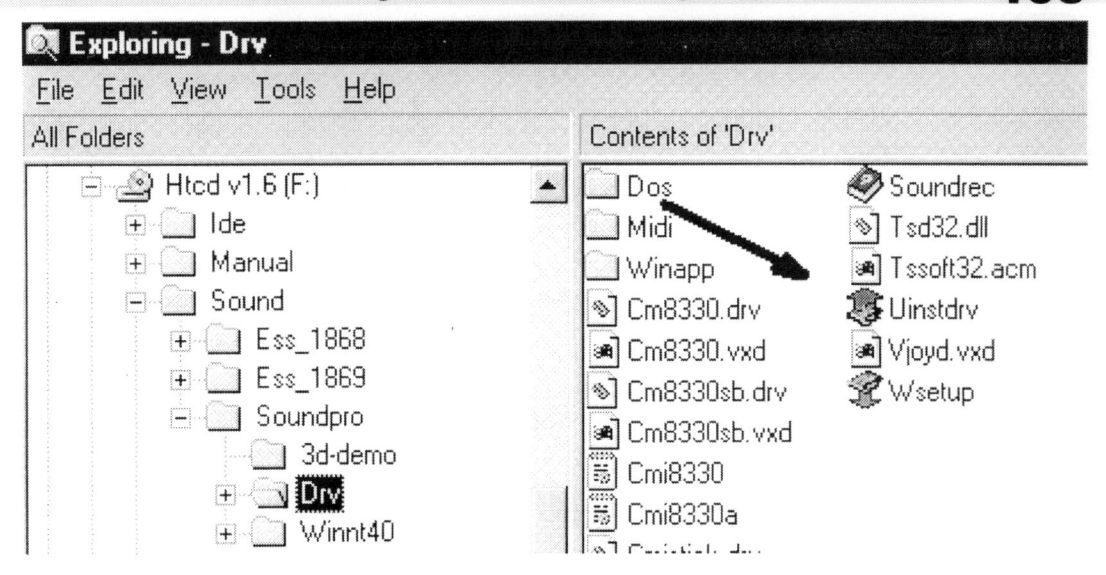

INSTALLING MODEMS

All modems nowadays are compatible with the PnP standard which makes their installation similar to a sound card. Just fit the modem into an available slot on the motherboard and Windows will detect it automatically, and begin loading the new hardware installation assistant, almost the same as for the installation of a sound card. During the process, you supply the information about where to find the drivers.

If you are using a hardmodem, it will be possible to disable the Plug-and-Play and configure the IRQ and address you want to use manually. You may do this by altering the position of some jumpers found on the modem card itself. The layout and jumper settings should be found in the modem's manual and in many cases on the modem as well.

154 HARDWARE PC

A. Standard Communication Port selection

S1	COM 1	COM 2	IRQ 3	IRQ 4	PNP OFF 5	ADDRESS, IRQ
COM1	Close	Close		Close	Close	3F8-3FF, IRQ4
COM2		Close	Close		Close	2F8-2FF, IRQ3
COM3	Close			Close	Close	3E8-3EF, IRQ4
COM4			Close		Close	2E8-2EF, IRQ3

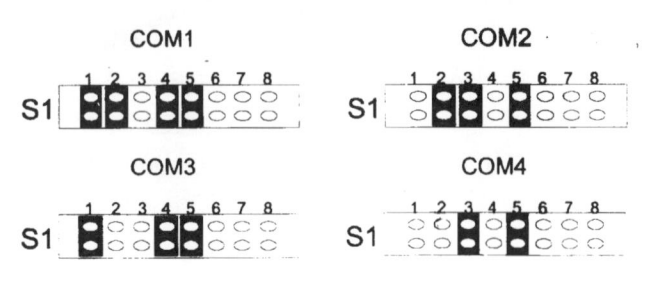

B. Plug and Play Setup (Plug and Play)

In the case of softmodems, you will not find any jumpers at all, but depending on the model, the driver program **"Hspcfg"** installed for it may permit you to alter the IRQs etc of the modem by using the Control Panel).

The installation of a PnP modem will often cause a device in computers that have few available addresses. If this happens you should configure the modem to use another address manually. Modems use a COM port and an IRQ address. There are four serial COM ports in most computers and COM 1 is usually occupied by the mouse. Configure the modem to use another port. Note that the COM 1 and COM 3 ports share the same IRQ (IRQ 4) whilst both COM 2 and COM 4 share IRQ 3. To avoid conflicts, if the mouse is installed on COM 1, configure the modem to use COM2 or COM 4 which use a different IRQ.

You can change the address that the mouse uses through the Setup. Access the **"Integrated Peripherals"** menu. There you can set the addresses used by the motherboard for the two serial ports (Onboard Serial Port 1 and Onboard Serial Port 2). If you are not using the second port, its is a good Idea to disable it to avoid future conflicts.

Remember that if you manually configure the address of the modem it no longer becomes Plug-and-Play. To install the modem you should enter the Control Panel and click on the "Modems" icon. Execute the modems installation wizard. Windows will then search all the installed COM ports in order to detect your modem.

If Windows doesn't have suitable drivers, it will be detected as a "standard modem". Then click on the "Change" button and choose the manufacturer supplied drivers. If you don't have the modem drivers, install it as "Standard 28000 bps modem", "Standard 33600 bps modem" or "Standard 56000 bps modem", whichever is closest to your modem speed.

You also need to disable Plug-and-Play to install your modem in operating systems that don't support this standard, like Linux.

INSTALLING PRINTERS

To install your printer in Windows 95/98 click on My Computer, Printers and the Add new printer. The installation assistant will then start. Click on the Next button and a menu will appear listing various printer drivers. If case your printer is not shown on the list, click on the "Have disk" button and install the manufacturer supplied drivers.

During the installation, Windows will ask in which logical port the printer should be installed. Unless you have installed a printer in a second parallel port or are using a serial printer, you should choose the port LPT1.

In many cases you only have to execute an installation program on a manufacturer supplied disk, with most CDs they will autoinstall just by placing the CD in the drive.

Installation program for a HP690 printer, downloaded from the manufacturers site,

INSTALLING SCANNERS

Installation of Scanners is summed up by the installation of standard TWAIN driver ("Tecnology Without Any Interesting Name").

This is not really a "Driver" as such, just a manner of speaking, because the TWAIN "Driver" is a small program that controls the scanner. TWAIN drivers facilitate our life greatly by permitting that the scanner be used from within any graphics application from the sophisticated Photoshop to the much simpler Windows Imaging, because the image is scanned by the TWAIN driver: the graphics program just opens the image as if it were any other image.

To install a TWAIN driver, just execute the installation program that comes on the CD or diskette supplied by the manufacturer. To use the scanner, use a graphics program such as Imaging, Photo Editor, Paint Shop Pro, Photoshop. etc) and choose the acquire image (from scanner) option.

The majority of scanners nowadays use the computer's parallel port, so the physical installation is done just by connecting the cable to this. The printer should then be connected to the "Printer" socket behind the scanner, which functions as a kind of extension. Other scanner models use SCSI controllers or even their own proprietary controllers. The installation of these controllers has no mystery to it, just use the "Add new hardware" option in the Control Panel and supply the manufacturers drivers in case Windows does not have any suitable device drivers.

INSTALLATION OF SCSI CONTROLLERS

A single SCSI controller permits the installation of several peripherals. An 8 bit controller supports the use of up to 7 peripherals, whilst a 16 bit controller permits the connection of up to 15. Each peripheral receives an ID that may be a number from 0 to 6 for 8 bit controllers and from 0 to 14 for 16 bit controllers. Two peripherals may not have the same ID, just as a modem cannot have an IRQ used by a sound card.

Just as an IDE HD has jumpers which permit it to be used as a Master, Slave, or Cable Select, a SCSI peripheral also has some jumpers which permit you to choose its ID. In case you install several SCSI devices on the same controller, the ID numbers do not need to be sequential.: An HD may use ID 1 and a CD-R ID 6 for example, the only rule is that two devices may not use the same ID number.

Ribbon cables are used to connect the peripherals to the controller. There are SCSI cables with 50 wires (used by 8 bit controllers) and 65 wire cables (used by 16 bit controllers). There are cables with from 2 to 15 plugs permitting up to 15 SCSI devices to be Daisy chained together (The maximum permitted by a 16 bit controller as one ID is reserved for use by the controller itself.). You should acquire a cable with a sufficient number of plugs for the devices to be installed,

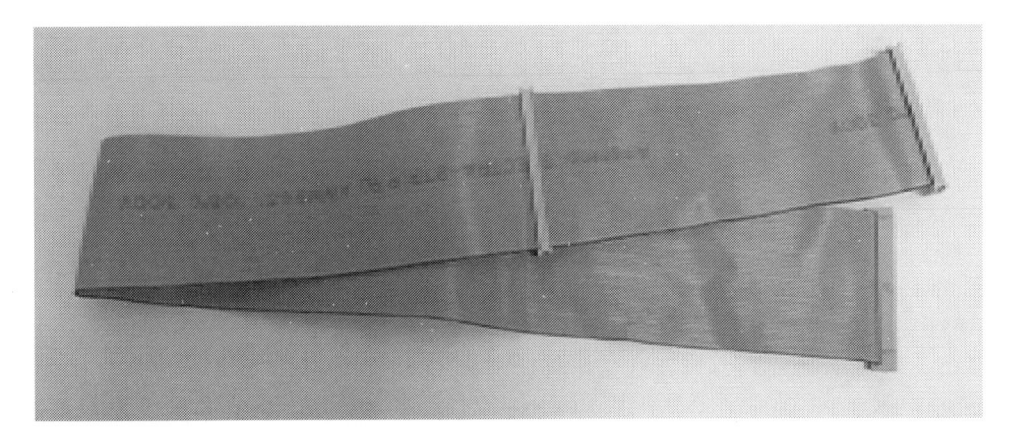

50 wire SCSI ribbon cable with three plugs that permits the installation of 2 SCSI peripherals.

For all the devices to function correctly, the last device should be installed with a terminator. This may be set through the use of jumpers, or by a plug, depending on the device. You will find instructions on how to do this in the device manual.

Every SCSI has its own BIOS that is initialized during the system boot-up. To access the Setup menu for the controller's BIOS which will permit you to set the IRQ to be used by the controller as well as any other options related to installed devices, you should press a certain key combination that will de displayed during it's initialization. In the case of the photo the key combination is Ctrl + A.

```
       AdvanSys PCI Ultra SCSI Bus Host Adapter BIOS v2.8M
              (c)Copyright 1997 Advanced System Products Inc.

Press <CTRL><A> to run AdvanceWare Utility

▶▶▶ AdvanSys PCI Ultra SCSI Bus Host Adapter Found At I/O Address 0x6100 ◀◀◀
    ID #0 : No Device Found
    ID #1 : No Device Found
    ID #2 : No Device Found
    ID #3 : SONY       CD-R    CDU948S    1.0g
    ID #4 : No Device Found
    ID #5 : No Device Found
    ID #6 : No Device Found
    ID #7 : AdvanSys Ultra SCSI PCI Bus Host Adapter
```

You should now install the controller drivers in Windows. In some cases you should execute a new hardware installation assistant using the Control Panel. In others you just have to execute a program contained on the cards installation CD that will install the drivers for you. In still other cases, Windows itself has suitable drivers for the card and will install them automatically.

USING THE DEVICE MANAGER.

To see all the installed devices and change the IRQ, DMA addresses etc, Windows offer the Device Manager. Access it through the "Control Panel", "System", and the "Device Manager".

The organization of the device manager is very similar to Windows Explorer and should be familiar to you. The devices are organized in categories such as "video cards", "network cards" etc. To see the devices, just double click on the corresponding category.

To see all the IRQ, DMA, I/O addresses and memory that is being used, click on the "Computer" icon and then on properties.

In the upper part of the window you can choose to exhibit the IRQ, DMA, I/O addresses and memory used.

This window serves only to show the addresses that are being used by a device. To alter a device's address, you should return to the main window, click on the device icon and then on the "properties" button.

In the window that comes up, choose menu "Resources" and unmark the "Use automatic configuration" check Box. Now just click on the resource you want to configure to open the corresponding windows.

Depending on which addresses you choose you will see various messages in the lower part of the window advising if there is a conflict of resources or if there are no conflicts. Every time conflicts appear you can try to alter the addresses used by the devices.

MAKING A SMALL NETWORK

More and more, businesses, as well as home users are discovering the advantages of connecting their computers to a network. After all, a network permits the sharing of printers, CD-ROMs, files and much more. It is much easier to use a network to print or copy files than to carry diskettes around; and instead of each computer having to have its own printer, CD-ROM etc, it is much cheaper to have only one of each and share them between all the computers.

To mount a small network of, say, from 3 to 5 micros is much easier than you may imagine. You don't need a server or hubs etc, only a network card for each computer and some coaxial cable.

The use of coaxial cable instead of twisted pair is ideal for small networks of up to 6 or 8 computers because it makes the installation simpler and cheaper because you don't need to use a HUB. Although coaxial cable may be used in larger networks from 8 or 9 upwards, twisted pair and hubs are better for these. The coaxial cable used in networks of computers is different from that used by TV antennas because it has a lower impedance (50 ohms instead of 75 ohms). We use cables called 10Base2 also known as fine coaxial cables which are especially for use in networks.

At the back of the network card you will find two sockets, one round called BCN and the other oblong called RJ-45. The BCN socket is used for the connection of coaxial cables whilst the RJ-45 socket is used by twisted pairs. You may only use one of these at a time.

The cables are made to order, according to the distance between the computers. You will find the cables and connectors in any good computer shop, many will make the cables on the spot according to the client's needs.

160 HARDWARE PC

You can also make your own cables. The coaxial cables are plugged into a BCN "T" connector which is then connected to the network card. Normally the network card comes with one of these "T" connectors but you can also buy them separately. To fit the cable to the plug you first need to strip them using suitable special wire-stripper for co-axial cables and then crimp them into the connector.

The minimum distance between each node (or computer on the network) is 50 cm and the maximum distance is 180 meters. At the two ends you should close the cable by using a 50 ohm terminating resistor. Usually shops that sell the cables will also sell the terminators and any necessary tools. (crimpers, strippers etc). As already mentioned, many make cables to order and you will not have any work to do apart from specifying the distances between the computers.

After the physical part of the network installation has been completed you just have to make Windows recognize the network cards and install the communications protocol and share the resources.

INSTALLING A NETWORK CARD

Almost all the network cards on sale are Plug-and-Play which means they will be recognized as soon as the computer is switched on. Just supply the drivers that come with the card (in case Windows does not have them in its library).

In case the card is not automatically detected, go to the Control Panel and then click on "Network". Click on the "Add:" button, choose adapter and then "Have disk" .

CONFIGURING THE NETWORK

In order for the computers to talk amongst themselves, it will also be necessary to install a network protocol. The protocol functions as a kind of interpreter permitting the computers to converse in the same language. Open the network icon again and click once more on "Add". In the menu that appears, click on "Protocol". Another menu similar to the add printers comes up. On the left side (manufacturer) choose "Microsoft" and on the right hand side (network protocols) choose "NetBeui".

When you click "OK" you will return the network configuration window. Click again on "Add" and now choose "Client". From the left hand menu choose "Microsoft" and "Client for Microsoft Networks" on the right hand side. Click on "OK" to finish.

Again go back to the network configuration window. Click on "Add", "Service",

"Microsoft" and finally on file and printer sharing for Microsoft Networks".

Return to the main menu, and click "OK" to close the network configuration window. You will be asked to supply the Windows installation files. Insert the CD or inform the location of the files.

After the computer has been reinitialized, you just have to share the resources that you want other computers on the network to use. To do this just click on "My Computer", right click over the HD, CD-ROM, disk drive etc you want to share, and choose sharing from the menu that pops up.

Change the option from "No sharing" to "Shared as". In the field "Shared name" give any name to the device and in the comments field you may write something to remind you what it is. In the "Access type" option you may choose between three options:

Read only : The other computers may only read the files on the disk, but they may not alter files, or copy anything to the disk.

Full : The other computers may have full access to the disk, they may copy, change, or delete files, exactly as if it was their own hard disk.

According to password : Permits you to establish access passwords. In this way the resource only can be accessed if the user of the other computer has a password. You can choose different passwords for full access and read only access.

Instead of sharing the whole disk to may choose to share only some folders. To do this, leave the hard disk as "Not shared" and share only the desired folders by right clicking above them and choosing shared.

 To share the printer, access the "printers" icon, right click above it and again choose "sharing". Share it, give it a name and if you wish, establish an access paaword.

Ready, now just switch on all the computers and the shared resources will appear in Windows Explorer or by opening the "Network environment" that is on the work desk. Everything that is shared may be accessed as if it were part of each computer.

REINSTALLING WINDOWS

In many problem cases it is simpler to give up and just re-install Windows than to spend hours trying to resolve a difficult problem. A badly written program may replace library files used by other programs when it installs itself, important files or even Windows registry might be damaged by a power cut teat reset the computer or even due to defects like bad memory contacts, just to name a few of the problems that come when you least expect them. If you have already tried everything to resolve a problem without success and come to the conclusion that there is no alternative except to re-install the operating system, then some tips might be useful.

There are two types of re-installation of Windows, complete and partial. A partial reinstallation means executing the installation program again and re-installing Windows in the same directory, above the original version. In this case you won't lose anything, all your programs continue functioning and all the configurations will be maintained, but the counterpart to this is that it doesn't always resolve problems because it leaves the Windows registry intact. This type of re-installation serves only to restore system files that have been accidentally deleted or to replace corrupted or damaged files, as long as you were aware which files had problems. However, on the other hand, a complete re-installation of the operating system will be capable of solving any type of problem, except, obviously, incompatibility problems, conflicts or hardware defects in the computer.

To re-install your Windows from scratch without needing to format the hard disk you just have to install it in a different directory from the other. If Windows was installed in the folder "Windows", install it to a folder "Win95" or "Win98" for example. To avoid any confusion rename your folder "Program files. When you have finished the installation and it is all functioning OK, delete the old Windows and Program Files folders., leaving only what you want, or can reuse on the hard disk.

12 F.A.Q.

Processors

I am thinking of buying a computer soon, but don't know whether to choose one with a K6-2, Celeron with cache, or a Cyrix 6x86 (the K6-3 and the Pentium III are too expensive for my budget). Although the principal use of this computer will be word processing and Internet, my son will use it a lot for games. Which processor would you indicate for me, taking into account that I cannot spend very much?

The Celeron A equipped with a 128Kb cache represents a drastic improvement over the Celeron without a cache. Although the Celeron A has a small quantity of cache, this functions at the same speed as the processor gives a performance which only just below a Pentium II. In fact the Celeron equals the Pentium II in graphics applications.

The K6-2 has a performance very similar to the Celeron A in Office applications, but loses in graphics applications and games due to weaker math co-processor its which is not as good as the Celeron or Pentium. The performance of the math co-processor is almost as important as the rest of the processor because this determines its ability to function with number fractions. Graphics programs and games with polygonal graphics (practically all that are sold nowadays) make intensive use of floating point calculations. A processor with a weak math co-processor would present a poor performance in these applications.

The Cyrix 6x86, in its turn presents a math co-processor almost 40% slow er than that of the K6-2, however even having 3D NOW instructions to compensate, its performance is weak in games and graphics programs that use a large number of floating point calculations. In spite of its drawbacks, the low cost compensates and the 6x86 would really only be indicated for Office type applications.

Meanwhile, the performance of the Celeron is not going to help much in games without a 3D video card. Do your sums and see with which configuration it would be possible to buy a 3D card, even if it was simpler. The ideal for games would be a Celeron but it is preferable to have a K6-2 with a 3D card than a Celeron without.

MOTHERBOARD

I have an ASUS motherboard with a chipset i430VX that according to the manual supports up to a Pentium 200. Actually I am using a Pentium 100 but am thinking of upgrading to a 233MMX I inherited. Will I have to change the motherboard?

The MMX instructions are only software This means that any motherboard capable of working with a normal Pentium also will work with an MMX processor, at least in theory. The problem is the voltage. Many older motherboards are not capable of supplying the 2.8 V used by MMX, and to install a MMX processor in a motherboard that is set to supply 3.3 or 3.5V will cause overheating and instability and may damage the processor.

Have a look in the manual and see if there is support for the 2.8V needed by the MMX. If there is then you can install the MMX without problems, you will just have to set the bus frequency for 66 MHz and the multiplier for 1.5x (wich this processor interprets as 3,5x). Check if there is also a jumper called "CPU Type". If there is, then it should be set to dual voltage or P55C.

I bought a used motherboard from a friend and installed an old Pentium 133 which was gathering dust to make a second computer. Whiles browsing the Setup I noticed that the L2 cache was disabled. But after I enabled it Windows began to lockup frequently. Is there anything I can do or will I have to put up with using a computer with the L2 cache disabled. (it is unbearably slow!)

Many times the L2 cache presents problems when we force it to work at a very high frequency. Try to enter into the Setup and re-enable the L2 cache, but also reduce its operating frequency through options like "Cache Timing" or "Cache Read Cycle" found in the "Chipset Features Setup" menu or a similar one. With this there is a good chance that the cache will function normally.

If the motherboard uses Coast memory cache modules, try removing them and cleaning their contacts with an eraser (vinyl type, not rubber) and replace it again carefully in the motherboard. You can also try it without the cache memory modules. In many cases the problem is only a bad contact.

My motherboard's CMOS battery (I have a rather old 486) is inside a black Box, a little big bigger than a small torch battery that is connected to the motherboard by a wire. I need to change this battery but can find nothing like it on sale.

Many older motherboards use this type of battery for the CMOS wich is no more than a 3 Volt battery inside a plastic casing connected to the motherboard by a wire. You can just open this plastic case and change the battery that is inside. You can also jerry-rig it with two small batteries (the cheapest solution) or then use a 3 volt camera battery which can be found in photographic shops. There are various models, some of them will fit within the plastic casing, just attach the wires (solder them if possible) to the new battery. These batteries cost 2 or 3 dollars.

HARD DISK AND MEMORY

I have a VX-PRO motherboard with 64 Mb 72 pin EDO memory. Can I add one more 32 MB Dimm memory module, enabling the jumper for DIMM and then keeping my 64 MB of memory EDO giving me a total of 96 MB?

In the majority of cases, 18 pin memories can be mixed with 72 pin memories without problems. Before buying the new memory, however, you should verify the number of memory banks that can be occupied simultaneously your motherboard which can support. Although they usually have 4 sockets for 72 pin memories and 2 for 168 pin memories, the majority of motherboards support only 2 or 2 occupied banks at the same time. This information may be obtained from the motherboard manual.

It is worth remembering also that motherboards that use the Socket 7 with the exception of those with a chipset i430HX and the newer Super 7 socket motherboards, are only capable of caching 64 Megabytes of RAM memory. A Windows uses the upper part of memory for caching, the use of more than 64Mb will make the performance of the system fall up to 40% in normal applications because for the majority of applications it would be as if there was no cache installed. The use of more than 64Mb is only justified in the case of programs that use all available RAM such as video editors or large image processing programs. This problem doesn't occur in computers equipped with a Pentium II processor because the cache controller is built into the processor itself and is capable of caching 512Mb or up to 4Gb depending on the series of the processor. Super 7 motherboards as used by the K6-2 and K6-3 also don't have this problem, caching 128Mb or 256Mb depending on the chipset that is used.

What is BUS Mastering? What is it used for?

BUS Mastering is a resource supported by some bus architectures which permits the disk controllers to communicate directly with the devices without using the processor. An HD with BUS Mastering drivers would be capable of accessing memory directly without resorting to the processor which, as well as improving the performance, doesn't use processing power, leaving it free to execute other tasks. UDMA HDs use Ultra DMA whilst Pio Mode 4 HDs use the Multiword DMA 2. In both cases you should install the BUS Mastering drivers that come with your motherboard in order to activate this resource. Windows 98 already has BUS Mastering drivers for the greater majority of motherboards, dispensing with the need for installation in most cases.

In dealing with hard disks, what is the difference between Multiword DMA 2 and UDMA? How can I enable them?

Traditionally the processor commanded the transfer of data from the hard disk to memory. This resulted in processor occupancy rates that could be more that 80% during transfers. Whilst a file was copied from one disk to another for example it was practically impossible to work with another program because everything was very slow. The loading time of programs was also greater because the processor, as well as having the task of having to open the program, also had to control the transfer of the necessary files to memory.

In order to solve this, we use DMA ("Direct Memory Access") so that the work of transferring data is executed by the chipset, leaving the processor free to execute other tasks. Multiword DMA 2 is the DMA used by Pio Mode 4 HDs, supported by all chipsets as from the i430FX. To enable it, just install the appropriate drivers.

You will find the "BUS Master IDE Drivers" on the installation CD which came with your motherboard and these should be installed. After the installation, enter into the device manager that is in the Control Panel, click on the hard disk icon at the bottom then the setup menu and check the DMA option to enable it. Windows 98 already comes with BUS Master drivers for the majority of motherboards and in most cases it is not necessary to install them when using Windows 98.

UMDA is the current standard for hard disks, permitting data transfers at 33Mb and implementing a type of DMA a little more efficient than Multiword DMA 2. Again Windows 98 already has the necessary drivers for the majority of motherboards. In case you are using Windows 95, install the drivers that came with the motherboard.

If you have lost the drivers CD for your motherboard you can find the drivers on Internet, in your motherboard manufacturer's site. If it is equipped with an Intel chipset you may also use the generic drivers supplied by Intel, which may be downloaded from Intel's site: **http://intel.com/support/chipsets**.

In the site **http://www.ping.be/bios/** you can download a program called ctbios.exe which identifies the manufacturer of your motherboard and supplies the address of its site on Internet.

After a bit of hesitation I finally decided to make my own DIY computer. However I have got problems in installing the operating system. I installed the HD as the Master on the Primary IDE and Auto detected it in the BIOS Setup, but when I give a boot by diskette and try to access the HD, I can't manage to access it, and it appears as if there was no hard disk installed!

You forgot an important part of the process: the partitioning and formatting of the hard disk :-) Get a boot disk for Windows 95 or 98 and after booting the computer with this, execute Fdisk by typing the command A:\FDISK. Partition the disk as you want, exit the program and re-boot the computer using the same boot disk. Now use the Format command to format your hard disk and it will be ready for use. In case you created more than one partition, each one has to be formatted separately, using the commands Format C: , Format D: , Format E: , etc.

After falling on the floor (it slipped), my HD began to present several bad blocks, being marked as such by Scandisk. A friend told me that I could install this disk in an old 386 or 486 motherboard that had the HDD Low Level Format option and do a physical low level format of the hard disk, and that the bad blocks would disappear. Would this really work?

This Low-Level Format option found in older motherboard Setups is aimed at the older HDs based on the ST-506 and ST-412 standards that predated the hard disks used nowadays. These disks were much simpler than the current ones, so that the physical formatting was done by the user himself through the Setup. As well as this, these disks needed o be reformatted physically due to misalignment problems caused by the expansion and contraction of the magnetic surface with temperature and a lack or precision in the stepper motor that was used to move the read heads.

In these disks the quantity of sectors per track was the same in the outer tracks and in the inner tracks (as in diskettes) being very easy for BIOS to determine the correct number of tracks and sectors on the disk and do the physical formatting. The Low Level Format option is found even is some relatively recent 486 motherboards just in order to maintain compatibility with the obsolete disks.

Current disks using the IDE and SCSI standards however use a resource called Zoned Bit Recording that uses a more rational division of space, permitting the outer tracks, which have a greater circumference to have more sectors than the inner tracks. Due to this feature it is extremely difficult to determine with precision how many sectors each track has in order to do a physical format because the number varies from track to track. Current disks don't suffer from the problem of track misalignment found in the obsolete ST disks, and therefore any attempt at physical formatting is unnecessary and completely inadvisable, because it would be very difficult for BIOS to recognize the tracks and sectors precisely and if the format was executed with incorrect parameters the disk may be rendered unusable. In the majority of cases it will refuse to format the disk and give an error message.

When a hard disk diagnostic program like Scandisk which comes with Windows 95 and 98 is executed, it tests all the sectors on the hard disk and marks any damaged ones in a reserved area of the disk called the Defect Map so that they are no longer used. These defective sectors are also called bad clusters or bad blocks.

These sectors are marked as defective exactly because they present a tendency to have data corrupted when recorded. A physical format of the hard disk would also erase the Defect Map, making these sectors being seen as good again by the operating system. This desperate attempt would not solve the problem, it would simply make the damaged areas of the disk (previously marked as damaged) return to be used and that would certainly end up causing corruption in data that was recorded to the disk.

I was given an old 1.2 Gigabyte HD as a present from a friend who made an upgrade in his computer. The problem is that when I ran Scandisk it began to mark several disk sectors as having defects. I though that the problem was resolved but every time I run Scandisk it marks sectors with defects, all towards the end of the disk. What can I do to guarantee more security for data I record on this disk?

There must have been some shock to this disk during transport or handling which damaged some areas of the magnetic disk. As it seems that a large area of the disk was damaged, Scandisk is having problems correcting it.

What happens is that before marking a cluster as defective, it tries several times to recover the data recorded there, and if after several attempts the data is recovered, it considers that the cluster is still recordable and does not mark it as defective. When Scandisk is run again, it maybe that this same cluster, whose data had previously been recovered, fails completely after several attempts and is marked as being defective. This is what appears to be happening with you due to there being a large damaged area on the disk.

In this case you may run Scandisk several times until it doesn't find any more damaged sectors (this may take a while :-) or then repartition the disk in such a way that the damaged area is not used. This last option offers a greater safety margin, in spite of losing a part of the usable disk area:

If your hard disk was formatted with a FAT 16 it should have approximately 38.000 clusters. As the damaged clusters are appearing only at the end of the disk, run Scandisk once more and note where it begins to find the bad clusters. You won't have any difficulty noticing as Scandisk will start to go much more slowly than normal due to the fact that it is trying several times to read these areas.

Very well then, suppose that the damaged clusters started appearing after block 35,000 for example. This divided by 38000 is approximately 92%. You can then run Fdisk, delete the current partition and create a new partition using only 90% of the total disk space (leaving the 2% as a safety margin). The other 8% damaged will not be used, just the good 90% and you should not have any more problems with bad clusters.

In some cases the damaged area is at in the beginning of the disk. As Fdisk only permits you to create partitions from the beginning, then create a partition covering the defective area (that won't be used) and another that covers the rest of the disk. Another solution would be to use a better partitioning program that offers the option of creating a partition as from the end of a disk. A good program is Partition Magic from Power Quest.

I would like to know which is the best option for gaining more space on an HD: Use a FAT 32 or a compacting program such as Drivespace? Which of the two solutions is most recommended? I have heard that Fat 32 reduces the performance of the computer a little in relation to Fat 16. If this is so, would I have any advantages in compacting it using DriveSpace?

The only way to finish with a lack of space on an HD is not to use the computer seriously though, you can obtain good space saving by using FAT 32 because it takes better advantage of the space, and you can expect a considerable saving of around 15% to 40%. But for the larger number of clusters to be

170 HARDWARE PC

managed by the operating system the access speed falls a little, around about 3%, which, however you look at it, is imperceptible.

I do not recommend the use of drivespace nowadays because it substantially reduces the performance of the disk and the system as a whole as well as the fact that the processor is always having to decompact data coming from the Hd before it can be copied to memory and then compact it again before it can write any data to the hard disk. There is also a greater chance of losing files and the problem of incompatibility. It is worthwhile remembering that you cannot compact a disk that has been formatted with a FAT 32.

I have a 1.08Gb Quantum Fireball HD and I am getting a 6.4Gb Quantum Fireball EX UDMA which I am going to install together in my PII. My doubt is whethee the 1.08 GB Hd that is much slower will influence the performance of the other.

You can use the two HDs in the same computer without problems, however in order not to degrade the performance, one should be on the primary IDE controller, and the other on the secondary IDE controller. I would suggest the new 6.4 as a Master on the Primary IDE controller, and the old one as a Master on the secondary controller, with the CD as a salve on this secondary controller. If the two were on the same controller there would be a small loss of performance.

I bought a 4.3Gb HD but when I formatted it there was only 3.9 GB. Why?

A Kbyte has 1024 bytes, a Megabyte has 1024 Kbytes and a Gigabyte has 1024 Megabytes. The manufacturers have a habit of rounding these values down to 1000 as it makes their HDs appear larger. Your HD does not have 4.3 Gigabytes but 4,300,000,000 bytes, which if expressed correctly in Megabytes is slightly less than 4.0Gb.

I made the mistake of connecting the power cable the wrong way round in my HD, that is, 12V where there should have been 5 volts and 5 instead of 12V! I really need to recover the data that is in this HD, is there any way I can make it function again. ?

In your case you will have burnt out the logic board of your HD, however your data continues to be intact on the magnetic disks within it. You will have to lookout for computer scrap merchants or repair shops until you find a logic board the same as yours to buy. It may be a little difficult to find, but if you do to you will get your HD back by changing this board. If your HD is fairly new, another possibility is to buy a new one of the same make and model and use the logic board from this.

My computer is a 486DX4-100, I have one 16Mb memory module in one of the 72 pin sockets. When I try to install another 4Mb 72 pin memory module the computer boots up OK and runs DOS applications, games etc. normally. But when I try to start Windows 95 it gives an error message about memory and hangs up, or sometimes says "Your computer may be safely switched off". What can I do to make Windows run with this 4Mb?

The memory is damaged, or there is some incompatibility between the modules. In any case, it is a hardware problem. Try changing this 4Mb for another, or leave it with 16MB as 4Mb will not make much difference. Windows is much more demanding with memory than DOS and, as well as this, it accesses memory from the top down, that is, it will access the 4Mb first and only after this is used will it access the 16MB. If there is a problem with the 4Mb, it will lock up early in the initialization process, showing an error message with the faulty memory address. If you swap the memory modules you may note that Windows initializes normally as it begins accessing the 16Mb first.

When you begin to use other applications and the 4Mb starts being used, errors will begin to appear. The last possibility is that your 4Mb is EDO memory as the majority of 486 motherboards don't accept this type of memory.

OTHER PERIPHERALS

I had an interesting situation: I assembled a K6-2-300Mhz with a 6.4Gb HD, multimedia and modem in an AT case that had a power supply of 250Watts. The computer reinitialized by itself, and sometimes didn't even switch on. I changed the power supply for another 300W one and the problems disappeared. Was it that the old 250W power supply was not sufficient?

In your case, 250W should be more than sufficient as the motherboard together with the processor uses less than 30 Watts, an HD around 25W, a CD-ROM drive around 30, a 32 MB of memory consumes about 15W, a sound card about 10W and a disk drive uses less than 10 watts.

Altogether, your computer needs about 120 watts that is amply covered by a 250 watt power supply or even a 200W one. The monitor, even when connected to the socket in the power supply doesn't come into the picture because this is only an extension of the power in socket.

The problem with many low quality power supplies is that they are nor capable of supplying a constant flow of current, which may be aggravated by a poor mains supply. I believe that your problem was caused by this, a low quality power supply. If you had changed it for another of 250Watts or even 200W of better quality you would not have had problems. Also what happens is that as a power supply gets older the electrolytic filer capacitors dry out causing exactly the same problem.

I have decided to buy a 3D and as I cannot spend very much, decided on a Viper V330. In the shop where I am going to buy it they have both AGP and PCI versions, both with 4Mb of memory. The PCI version is a little bit more expensive. Is there any difference between the two? Why is the PCI version more expensive?

If a video card uses the AG bus it can use RAM memory to store textures when the video card's memory runs out with a greater speed than the PCI bus. Another advantage of AGP is that it has a greater data bandwidth, 266Mbs as compared with only 133 MB/s of the PCI.

A Viper V330 is a low cost video card that has a good cost benefit ratio, but it has no great advantage over the AGP bus because it is not fast enough to manipulate large quantities of textures and by the fact that the flow of data it is capable of sending to the processor would be dealt with equally, as well as by a 133Mb PCI version. In this case, the PCI version and the AGP one have a similar performance, that does not happen with faster cards where the use of AGP makes a big difference.

If your motherboard has an AGP slot, give preference to the AGP version of the Viper. But if you do not have an AGP slot, you will have to opt for the PCI version, but there will not be a great performance loss. I would imagine that the PCI version of the Viper is more expensive because of the lower production quantities.

I recently bought a Viper V 330 3D video card but up until now I have not been able to get it to function adequately. Even by installing the drivers that came with the card, and others that I found on the manufacturers Internet site, I haven't been able to activate its 3D functions any way. Actually, even now, I haven't been able to configure a resolution of more than 640x480 with 16 colors! What is happening? Has my video card got a defect?

I have already seen other people with the same problems as you. The problem is that the Viper V330, as well as practically all the 3D accelerator cards, need an IRQ to function correctly. Some BIOSes are capable of automatically detecting if the card needs an IRQ and if so allocate one to it. In others this is determined by the user himself through the "Assign IRQ to VGA Card" or "Allocate IRQ to VGA Card" options that some BIOSes have in a menu similar to "PCI/Plug and Play Setup" or in others "Advanced CMOS Setup".

In the majority of cases, the motherboard is capable of automatically detecting the necessity of reserving an IRQ for the video card and in others this option is enabled by default in the Setup. It happens that some older motherboards manufactured before 96 or 97 have this option disabled by default, as at that time video cards which used this resource were quite rare. In this case the problem is solved simply by activating the option in the Setup.

I would like to understand better what determines the maximum values of the monitor refresh rate in Windows 98. I have Samsung 15 GLI monitor and a Viper V330 using the Nvidia Riva 128/128ZX drivers. Using a resolution of 1024x768 the maximum refresh rate I get is 75Hz. I would like to know if I could manage a higher refresh rate at this resolution as the values in the manuals of both the monitor and video card shoe values up to 120 Hz. Are these values only for lower resolutions?

Basically what determines the maximum refresh rate is the number of horizontal lines that the monitor is capable of tracing each second. This information is found in your monitor's manual, under "horizontal scan frequency". 14" monitors, for example, are generally capable of scanning at up to 50KHz. As a general rule, divide the number of horizontal lines that your monitor is capable of scanning per second by the quantity of horizontal lines desired, to know what will be the maximum refresh rate supported by the monitor at each resolution. A monitor that scans 50,000 lines per second, for example, will be capable of maintaining a refresh rate of 75Hz using a resolution of 800x600. At first sight it might seem that the maximum rate at 800x600 would be 83Hz given that 50.000 / 600 = 83, but there is a small loss due to the horizontal and vertical retrace. The time lost with retrace is approximately 5 or 6% depending on the monitor.

We could have, for example, a refresh rate of 75Hz (the image is renovated 75 times per second) in a monitor with 50,000 lines using 800x600 or 60Hz using 1024x768 (50.00 / 768 = 65), allowing for the retrace we arrive at approximately 60Hz.

I ended up buying an LG Studioworks 77i monitor. It seemed to me to be an excellent monitor with a good area of vision. But it seems to tire my eyes out more than my old Syncmaster 3. Is it only my initial impression, or is it an inherent characteristic in larger monitors.? What is the best resolution to work with using it? 800x600 or 1024 x 768? High Color or True Color? And as to the refresh rate, where do I adjust this and what is the best value? I should add that my video card is a Trident 9680 with 1 MB or memory.

The problem of tiredness in the eyes is caused by a low refresh rate. You should set the refresh rate to at least 75 MHz otherwise the screen will appear to shimmer and cause discomfort and in the long term may even damage your vision. In Windows 95/98 you can do this in the video properties within the control panel. However, for this you should have installed the correct driver for your video card.

The most common resolution in large monitors is 1024 x 768 or more, however this depends on personal tastes. It is worth remembering that with only 1Mb of video memory you will only be able to use 256 colors at a resolution of 1024 x 756, a good idea being to change the video card for one with 4MB. If you do not want to invest much in a new video card two good options are the Trident 9750 (cheapest) and the Viper V330 (with 3D resources). If you want a better performance buy a Viper V550 that is a little more expensive than the V330 but has a much superior performance. There is quite a difference between 16 bit color and True Color because 16 bits of color correspond to only 65,000 colors. Seeing a good quality color photo, the difference between them, leaps out before your eyes.

How do 3D sound cards work? What is their advantage over normal cards?

A 3D sound card is capable of generating sound effects in three dimensions that gives a much more realistic sensation to games. By using a card like this in compatible games you can hear sound coming from all sides and interesting effects makes which it much more real.

The oldest technique for the general use of three dimensional sound effects was Dolby Digital used also in Home Theaters which require the use of 6 strategically placed loudspeakers. The most modern technologies in use are Direct Sound 3D and Aureal 3D used in the majority of sound cards nowadays. These two technologies permit the use of three dimensional effects using a pair of normal loudspeakers, that as well as being more practical, lowers the cost of the equipment. 3D sound cards like the Turtle Beach Montego and Sound Blaster Live can be founds for sale for less than $80.

I have read some reports about the pros and cons of leaving the computer switched on always, like a refrigerator. Some state that this may even prolong the life of the computer, however, increasing energy consumption. Others say that constantly switching the computer on and off may even damage the peripherals. I am thinking of leaving mine switched on all the time seeing that I have Windows 98 Energy Star, and use my computer a lot, especially for Internet.

Is it really safe to leave my computer switched on the whole time, even if there are power cuts sometimes? I have a stabilizer but don't know if it supports voltage peaks. Would energy consumption increase a lot? Is this good for my HD and other peripherals.?

If you have Energy Star enabled the computer will automatically be put into minimum consumption mode, because after some time without use the components, including the monitor, are put into stand-by mode. The biggest problem in leaving the computer switched on 24 hours would be that it is more vulnerable to voltage surges and lightning etc, but this can be overcome by using a good no-break with some autonomy and a correctly installed earth. Keeping the computer switched on always may even increase its useful life because as in any electronic device, most wear occurs at the moment of switching on/off and not during the actual use.

IS THERE A DIFFERENCE IN SPEED BETWEEN SCSI SCANNERS AND THOSE THAT USE THE PARALLEL PORT??

Without any doubt, a SCSI controller permits a much faster passage of data than the parallel port of the computer, but as to whether the scanner can make use of this is another thing. Actually some of the fastest domestic scanners use the parallel port. This doesn't mean that the parallel port is faster, but in the case of a domestic scanner of 300 or 600 dpi (optical resolution), the transfer rate permitted by the parallel port is more than sufficient. The bottleneck is the time required to actually scan the image.

I want to buy a CD-ROM burner (recorder) soon but am indecided as to whether to buy an IDE or a SCSI model. In advertisements SCSI recorders are always more expensive. Is there any real advantage in the use of SCSI? Does the SCSI controller card come with the recorder or do I have to buy this separately?

The principal requirement for a CD-ROM recorder is a Constant flow of data from the hard disk. Any interruption in this flow would cause a buffer under-run, a situation where the recorder has used up all the data in its buffer without having received any new data from the HD, thus causing an interruption in the recording and the consequent loss of the CD being recorded. The use of a SCSI interface helps to reduce this problem a great deal, also with the advantage of leaving your IDE interfaces free for the installation of other peripherals, and therefore SCSI is strongly recommended for CD recorders. Usually a simple controller card is supplied together with the recorder as this doesn't increase its resale price much as they are relatively cheap. But this is not a hard and fast rule, check with your reseller.

After some 6 months of use my HP 692C printer began to show a loss of printing quality, being smudged and with several horizontal dotted lines, as if someone had scratched it with their fingernails before the ink had dried. I have already tried changing the cartridges twice, tried other types of paper, cleaned the cartridges etc, but the marks continue. It is interesting to note that this only happens when I am using the black cartridge, and doesn't happen in colored pages.

By what you have described it seems to me that the problem is only dirt in the cartridge trolley. This is a bit hard to clean as the space is very small. Try using cotton wool buds impregnated with pure alcohol or even a needle with a bit of cotton on the end.

Switch on the printer and lift the lid so that the print cartridges park themselves in the middle. Remove the power cable (with the printer still switched on) and remove the cartridges. Now just clean the area of this cartridge trolley which is close to the print heads of the cartridges and close to where the paper passes. Be insistent, sometimes the dirt and flecks of paper etc are hard to remove., a small pair of tweezers sometimes helps.

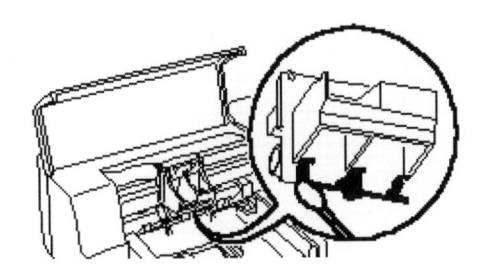

After I installed my modem, every time I switch on my computer their is a message appearing on the screen saying that there is a conflict in port 2F8, and asking me to pres F1 to enter in Setup. How can I remove this bothersome message?

By default the serial port 2 of your motherboard uses COM 2 with a logical address of 2F8. Your modem must be using the same address causing a conflict.

To solve the problem, just enter in the Setup and change the address of serial port 2 through the "Onboard Serial Port 2" option that may be in the "Integrated Peripherals" screen of the Setup. If you don't use this port then you may simple disable it.

I have an NE 2000 compatible network card and would like to know what the socket on it is, the one similar to the socket on the motherboard called BIOS, and what is the purpose of this?

This socket permits the installation of a "Boot EPROM", a type of flash memory, or ROM that permits the micro to boot from the server without having to have a hard disk or diskette. Until a short time ago it was the fashion to use networks where only the server had a hard disk, and all the terminals accessed data on the server. This concept permitted cheaper workstations (as they did not need hard disks) and functioned well when the network, used only text based applications, because in this case the data flow is relatively small permitting a server to control several workstations with an acceptable speed. It would not be possible to run any heavier programs such as Windows 95 for example, as the server would be overloaded due to the enormous data traffic.

I have a problem of overheating in my computer. Every time I try to play a heavy game the computer resets in the middle of the game, almost predictably, after about 10 minutes of playing. I know it is a problem of overheating because when it is cold, or the air conditioning is switched on I can play for as long as I like without any problems. However I cannot leave the air conditioning switched on all day long and would like to know if there is a cheaper solution for this problem.

During the last summer heat wave I had 5 clients with the same problem of overheating. The solution is to use a little heat conducting grease between the processor and the cooler and install a ventilator in the front of the computer case.

You can find burnt out power supplies for a few dollars in computer scrap dealers. Just remove the ventilator and connect the red and black wire to one of the plugs which come from the power supply in the computer. With this functioning as an exhaust, the processor will be much cooler. If you want you may install one more to the side of the processor to improve the ventilation even more.

Upgrade

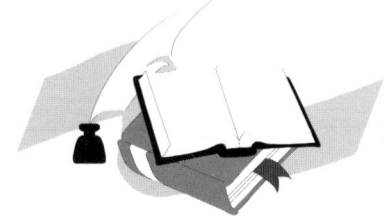

I have a Pentium 233 MMX with 32 MB EDO memory, 2.1 GB Quantum BigFoot HD, 16X CD-ROM and a Sound Blaster sound card. I want to make an upgrade in this computer but don't know whether to change the HD for a 6.4 GB Quantum Fireball or to change the processor and motherboard for a 350Mhz K6-2. I can only do one or the other because I don't have much money. I use the computer for Word, Excel, Internet and sometimes for games.

Your computer has a modest configuration, but it is still sufficient to run almost any application. The weak point is the hard disk that is very slow. Even if you don't have a lack of hard disk space, I would recommend changing the HD instead of the processor. The hard disk is of fundamental importance for the performance of the computer under Windows, because it determines the time needed to load Windows, load programs, open and close files, among other things. With a slow disk, everything is slower, quite apart from the processor speed.

Another favorable point in replacing the HD is that it would be easier to sell for a good price than the motherboard and processor. Part of the money from the sale could be used to buy another 3Mb of memory. With 64MB of RAM and a fast HD the performance of your computer will increase much more than if you had changed the processor.

I have a 486 DX-4 100 with 8 MB of memory, an HD with 520 MB, 1MB VLB video card and a VGA color monitor. In spite of the fact that I already have a better micro, I want to let my small children use this. What do you suggest that I change in this computer to obtain a reasonable performance running Windows 98 without spending much?

The first thing I would suggest is to install another 16Mb of memory. When running Windows 95/98 the quantity and speed of memory is more important than the processor, because with little memory Windows runs all the programs using the hard disk as virtual memory, that under-utilizes the processor, limiting the computer to the performance of the hard disk.

With 24Mb of memory this computer would be capable of running Windows 98, Office 95 or even 97 and the majority of games made until 2 or 3 years ago at a reasonable speed. In case you don't want to run Windows 98, the performance would be better still with Windows 95, that demands less from the computer.

As the computer is destined towards children, I would recommend the installation of a multimedia kit. If you don't want to spend much, you can assemble your own "kit". With less than $80 you can by a 48X CD-ROM, a basic sound card and loudspeakers (end of 1999).

I have an IBM Aptiva K5 100 MHz. Its motherboard has two sockets to add and cache memory modules. The specification is as follows: 160 pins, 64 bits, 256 (32Kx64), 15ns, asynchronous SRAM, 32Kx8, Tag SRAM. I would like to install two of these modules so that I would have a 512K cache. I could not find them in IBM's Site, do you know where I can buy them?

You should find these in an authorized IBM service center. Even so it is a bit difficult, and when you find them it will be for a rather absurd price.

You may also search in specialized computer shops for memory modules with these specifications, and these should function. In any case it would be easier and cheaper to change the whole motherboard for one with a cache of 512KB. With the popularization of the Pentium II and the super 7 motherboards you should find used socket 7 boards or even new ones for a good price and you may earn some pocket money from the sale of your old board. You can change the motherboard now and in the near future take advantage of it to change the processor as well.

I am using a Pentium 200 (without MMX) 48 Megabytes or memory and a 2.6GB HD. Do you think my computer will be good for another year, or should I think about an upgrade?

Well, you should know the answer to this yourself. A computer with this configuration is still sufficient to run the programs that an average user needs, such as word processors, spreadsheets, Internet and not so new games. If you use this computer only for this type of thing and are happy with its performance, then there is no need to make an upgrade. However, if you are planning to work with images, video, desktop publishing, or run some of the newest games, then it is time to make a change.

I know people that up until today run Windows 3.11 and Word 6.0 in 386 or 486 computers and are happy with their performance. The ideal configuration of a personal computer depends on the applications with which you are going to work.

I work with desktop publishing using mainly Corel Draw and Photoshop. I am suffering with a miserable 166 MMX with 64 Megabytes of memory, a 2.6GB HD, Trident 9685 video card with 4 MB and a 14" SVGA monitor. I want to make an upgrade using my holiday pay. What would you recommend for me in terms of cost benefits? Would you suggest buying a 3D video card?

You haven't said exactly how much you have to spend, but in terms of cost benefits I would suggest changing the motherboard and processor for a 433 or 466 Celeron (which presents a performance almost equal to the Pentium II but for half the price) and 128Mb of SDRAM memory.

Even if you are not needing more disk space it would be a good idea to change the hard disk for a faster one, which would also give a reasonable increase in overall performance.

You should also consider changing the monitor for a larger one that would be of great benefit by increasing your work area. Nowadays 17" monitors can be found for less than $300. In your case a 3D video accelerator is totally unnecessary but if you have any money left over and still want to invest in the computer, a combo 3D video card like the Viper V550 that is not too expensive would be a good idea, because as well as giving better 2D performance than your present card it, would let you place some 3D games during your leisure hours.

I am in doubt about the installation of a 3D Monster 2 video card. Does this need to have a normal 2D video card installed also? In this case I would have two video cards installed. Wouldn't this cause conflicts? Would I need some kind of adapter?

A Monster 2 as well as all 3D Stand Alone video accelerators only perform the 3D functions, so you also need to have 2 normal 2D video cards installed which will be responsible for the processing of two dimensional images. The video accelerator is installed in a free PCI slot and a cable is connected from the video output of the normal video card to a special input on the accelerator whilst the monitor is then connected to the 3D cards output. It is not necessary to have any special hardware and the cable comes together with the 3D card.

After the physical installation of the card you should install the drivers that accompanied it and also DirectX (In case it hasn't been installed.). To install the drivers you just have to execute an installation program that comes on the CD with the card.

Your old 2D card and the Monster 2 will function in parallel as if they were a single card and there is no possibility of conflicts.

WINDOWS

After installing some programs, Windows 95 began to hang up a lot. I tried to reinstall Windows in the same directory but this didn't help. I thought about a total reinstallation but don't want to format my HD. Is there any other way?

Yes, you can simply install Windows in another directory. Sometimes when you install new programs they replace shared DLLs used by other programs. This can cause instability and hangups. To try to find out which are the affected files and which registry entries should be altered is a very laborious task.

In these cases, re-installing Windows, while not being the ideal solution, is the simplest way out. Just re-installing Windows on top of the old copy doesn't resolve the problem as the registry, and the majority of files remain unaltered. The thing to do is install a "fresh" copy of Windows. To do this without needing to format the HD start Windows normally and rename the Programs files and Windows folders and execute the installation program with leaving Windows (just to facilitate access to the installation files). In case you want to re-install Windows 98 you should execute the installation program from DOS.

During the installation you will be asked in which folder you want Windows to be installed. Renamed the Windows folder, you may install it wherever you want, including in the Windows folder. When the installation is finished, just delete the old Program files and Windows folders as well as any others that you don't want any more, leaving only those that you want to use.

This procedure should resolve your problems without the necessity of erasing all your old files, but you will have the task of reinstalling all your programs again as well as some hardware.

F.A.Q. **183**

I have a computer with a Pentium 133 processor, 32 MB of memory, a 1.7GB formatted with a FAT 16 and Windows 95 installed. What do I need to do to install Windows NT 4 in this computer? Do I need to format the hard disk? I have been told that Windows NT 4 is much heavier than Windows 95 and that it doesn't run many programs. Is this true? Is it possible to keep Windows 95 even after installing windows NT?

Windows NT 4 uses a different filing system to Windows 95/98 called NTFS. In spite of this it is also compatible with Fat 16. The easiest way of installing Windows NT is from within Windows 95 itself. Just start Windows 95 normally and from there execute the NT installation program and install it in another folder, C:\WinNT, for example A boot manger will then be installed and you will be asked which system you want (NT or 95) to use every time that you switch the computer on. It is worth remembering that by leaving both in dual boot, each system functions independently from the other, you can even delete the Windows 95 folder and NT will continue functioning normally and vice versa.

Although there is no problem in installing NT in the same partition of a hard disk as Windows 95, it would be highly recommended to install it in a separate partition in order to keep everything better organized, and not mix programs used by both.

NT is much more stable and robust than Windows 95/98 because it is exclusively a 32 bit environment and doesn't permit programs to access the hardware directly. The areas of memory used by each program are allocated by the operating system that avoids a program using an area of memory used by another which would cause system crashes. It is really very difficult to cause Windows NT 4 to hang up, even on purpose.

This stability however has a price. 16 bit programs run under an emulator which as well as impairing their performance, makes NT incompatible with many older 16 bit programs. Other programs, especially games that rely on accessing the hardware directly will not run. You will never run a game that uses DirectX in Windows NT for example. Programs like Office, Corel Draw, Photoshop, Netscape, Internet Explorer and the majority of programs for 95 however, run without problems.

NT is also a little bit heavier than Windows 95 principally in terms of memory requirements. The absolute minimum to run NT reasonably is 32 Megabytes but the recommended minimum is at least 48. In your system it would run reasonably well but it would be highly recommended to increase the memory to 64 MB as soon as possible.

I was making some tests with DriveSpace 3 in my HD that has 2 GB divided into two partitions of 1 GB each. After using the program, miraculously the space available in each partition increased to 2GB. Are these value, real? Are there any problems in using this software?

More or less real. When you compact a disk using DriveSpace Windows shows that you have double the capacity but this isn't really true. It functions like this, program files, BMP images, Word documents, or any files that may be compacted will occupy less space on disk because they will be compacted. However, zipped files programs, installation files, JPEG images or any files that are already compacted will continue occupying the same space as before.

The problem with compacting the hard disk is that the processor will also have the work of un-compacting the data before it can use them, and also to compact them again before re-recording them back to disk. This impairs the overall performance as you have seen. Another problem is that when using compaction, all the files are stored in a single compacted volume. This increases the possibility of the total loss of all the saved files because any problem may damage the compacted volume, making it unusable and with no possibilities of recuperation.

If you are going to use disk compaction I would suggest using the first partition normally to store Windows and its files, and the other to store programs and files that may be highly compacted, compacting only these. This would substantially increase your free disk space without much effect on performance and reliability. Remember that you cannot compact a disk formatted with a FAT 32.

I have assembled my new computer, but I haven't been able to install the sound. I have already tried the Have disk option, but Windows 95 does not detect anything. What can I do? The motherboard is a PCChips M 571 with onboard sound.

On the CD that comes with the motherboard in one of the directories of the sound drivers you will find a file called "unistdrv" (or something similar). Execute this file and re-initialize Windows and the sound card will be detected. Now you just have to inform (via Have Disk) where the sound drivers are to be found and it will be installed.

F.A.Q.

AFTER ASSEMBLING MY NEW COMPUTER AND INSTALLING WINDOWS 95 OSR/2 (I THOUGHT WINDOWS 98 A BIT HEAVY) THERE IS A DEVICE CALLED PCI-BRIDGE IN THE DEVICE MANAGER THAT HAS AN EXCLAMATION MARK BY IT INDICATING IT IS NOT INSTALLED PROPERLY. WHAT IS THIS DEVICE AND WHAT DOES IT DO, AND HOW DO I MAKE IT FUNCTION?

The PCI-Bridge is one of the chips which composes the chipset and controls the transfer of data from the HD using the UDMA mode. As the IDE UDMA interfaces arose after Windows 95 it does not have the drivers to enable it, even though it has been detected because it is Plug and Play. Even without enabling the PCI-Bridge your IDE interfaces will function normally, but with UDMA disabled.

The drivers necessary to make the PCI-Bridge function may be found on the motherboard drivers CD. As Windows 98 is more recent it already has the drivers to install this hardware and does not need any external drivers.

In case you have lost the CD of your motherboard, you can find the drivers on the motherboard manufacturer's internet site. In case it has an Intel chipset you can also use the generic drivers supplied by Intel that can be found in the site of Intel: **http://intel.com/support/chipsets**

At **http://www.ping.be/bios/** you can download a program called ctbios.exe that identifies the manufacturer of your motherboard and supplies its address on Internet.

I am thinking of changing my computer but want to keep the same hard disk as this is large enough for me. Can I simply remove the HD from my current computer and install it in the new one? Will I need to reinstall Windows?

When you installed both Windows 95 and 98 it detected all the installed hardware in the computer and configured itself to work with it. If you simply remove the HD that has Windows from one computer and put it in another, Windows will see that the hardware is different when it initializes, it is as if you woke up in the morning in the body of a stranger.

Happily, Windows itself has elements that are responsible for detecting the hardware of the new computer and this is the reason for which you will find lots of messages "New hardware detected" during initialization, and it also sometimes asks for drivers or the installation CD. This radical change however may result in several problems like hardware conflicts or a device not being recognized.

The safest way to transplant a HD from one computer to another is to go to the control panel and remove all the installed devices before removing it from the old computer. Then switch off the computer and put the hard disk in the other computer. This will force Windows to detect all the hardware again, and guarantee a smoother transition.

It is a good Idea to do this before any change of hardware in the computer. If you are going to change the video card for example, remove the driver for the old one first. This helps avoid many problems.

I am having lots of problems with lock ups in Windows, blue screens, illegal operations etc. Then as I had nothing important stored, I decided to reformat my HD and reinstall Windows to solve these problems. However even after reinstallation, the problems continue, what can it be?

In most cases Windows hangups are not caused by bugs in the software but by a defect in the computer hardware. The processor may be overheating, RAM memory or cache memory may be failing, the video card could have problems, among other possibilities.

In your case I think that the problem would be with your computer hardware seeing that the problems were not resolved with reinstallation of Windows. The first thing to check would be if the processor is not overheating. This easily causes erratic functioning.

As your motherboard has not got temperature sensors, use the "finger test". After the computer has been used for some time, open the case quickly (or leave it open) remove the cooler and put a finger on the processor. A processor functioning with a normal temperature permits you to place your finger on it without burning it for at least 10 seconds. If you can't do this then you need to provide better cooling for the processor, such as exhausters, better coolers etc (see the chapter on overclock in this book). If the problem is not overheating of the processor I would suggest entering in the Setup of your computer and disabling the L2 cache. If your problems disappear, you have found the cause. You can then return to the Setup and try to reduce the cache speed to see if it starts working normally with the refresh, and if you can't put up with the loss of performance due to the disabling of the cache, you may have to change the motherboard.

If the problem is not the L2 cache, the next suspect is RAM memory. Try to enter in the Setup and reduce to its minimum speed. If the hangups continue try to make a test by substituting the memory with other ones.

If there are no problems with memory, then another suspect is the video card. Try entering in the video properties and disable the graphics hardware accelerator. If the problems disappear, change the video card because without the accelerator the computer would be a lot slower.

After installing a driver diskette that came with my CD-ROM (IDE), when I enter the control panel Windows 95, a message is exhibited saying that my hard disk was placed in MS-DOS compatibility mode that reduces the performance of the computer. By accessing help I saw that this problem is caused by real mode drivers installed in the Windows initialization and realized that this had been caused by the driver diskette for the CD-ROM I had installed. My problem is that even removing all references to these drivers in my initialization files my HD continues operating in compatibility mode. A friend said I would have to reinstall Windows, what do I do?

This diskette which came with your CD-ROM brings the drivers to enable it to function in MS-DOS. As Windows 95/98 automatically recognize CD-ROM drivers connected to IDE interfaces of the computer, it is not necessary to use this diskette.

Real mode CD-ROM drivers, loaded in the initialization of Windows, force the system to operate in this compatibility mode. In this case a key entry is generated in the Windows registry called "NOIDE". The problem is that even removing all references to the real mode drives in the CONFIG.SYS and AUTOEXEC.BAT files, this key value is not always removed from the registry and the system continues in compatibility mode making the performance of hard disks absurdly slow as they accessed using DOS routines, instead of Windows device drivers. Happily, it is easy to remove the "NOIDE" key from the registry (you don't even have to reinstall Windows). Open Notepad and create a text file with the following: (Copyright 1992-1998 Microsoft Corporation)

```
[version]

signature="$CHICAGO$"

[DefaultInstall]

DelReg = Del_IDE.Reg

[SourceDisksNames]

55="Remove NOIDE","",1

[SourceDisksFiles]

NoIDE.INF=55
```

[DestinationDirs]

NoIDE.Files.Inf = 17

[NoIDE.Files.Inf]

NoIDE.INF

[Del_IDE.Reg]

HKLM,%Location%,NOIDE,,

[Strings]

Location="System\CurrentControlSet\Services\VxD\IOS"

Save the file as "NOIDE.INF" in any directory and install it, by right clicking above it and choosing the "Install" option. When the computer is reinitialized it will function in 32 bit mode.

BIBLIOGRAPHY

Books
Norton Peter, Peter Norton's Inside The PC, Premier Edition. Publisher Sams Publishing, 1995
Manuals
Partition Magic User Guide. PowerQuest Corporation 1994-96
Supero, 440LX Chipset, AMI BIOS Reference Manual, revision 1.1 - Supermicro Computer INC. 1998
Articles
The BIOS Survival Guide, version 5.4 - Co-Edited by Jean-Paul Rodrigue (rodrighj@ere.umontreal.ca) and Phil Croucher (100427.2731@compuserve.com)
Portions Copyright 1996, Jean-Paul Rodrigue

Portions Copyright 1996, Phil Croucher
Internet Sites

MEMORY RELIABILITY "Parity Questions Answered"
http://net.wpi.edu/ram/

3D Hardware Net
http://www.3dhardware.net

WIM's Bios Page
http://www.ping.be/bios/

PC Guide
http://www.pcguide.com

PC Webopaedia
http://www.pcwebopaedia.com

Tom's Hardware Guide
http://www.tomshardware.com

Intel's Web site
http://www.intel.com

AMD's Web site
http://www.amd.com

Cyrix Online
http://www.cyrix.com

Abit Home Page
http://www.abit-usa.com

ASUS
http://www.asus.com

Sci.Electronics. Repair FAQ

http://www.repairfaq.org/

Comparing Flat LCD and Traditional CRT Monitors

http://www.touchscreens.com/compare_lcd_crt.shtml

Quantum

www.quantum.com

NOTES:

Printing (direct-to-plate system) and binding by:
Gráfica e Editora Santuário
Rua Padre Claro Monteiro, 342 -CEP 12570-000 - Aparecida - SP - Brasil
http://www.redemptor.com.br/grafica/portug.html

F.A.Q.